# Flight of a Maverick

*In the Secret War Against Hitler*

Robert H. Fesmire

Foreword by William E. Colby

For interviews and other information:
Southern Publishers Group
Birmingham, AL
1-800-628-0903

ISBN: 1-886371-13-X

Library of Congress Catalog Card Number
95-60097

Eggman Publishing, Inc.
2909 Poston Avenue, Suite 203
Nashville, TN 37203
(615) 327-9390

# DEDICATION

To my wife:

After my Carpetbagger experiences during World War II, I had to make many adjustments when I returned to civilian life. I met Maureen upon re-entering Vanderbilt University after the war. I thought she was the most beautiful girl on the campus. It was a perfect time to fall in love with someone who would make my life most meaningful. Our love and happiness have continued to grow over the years.

# ACKNOWLEDGEMENTS

I would like to express my heartfelt thanks to the following people:

- Our Carpetbagger intelligence officer for always providing accurate flight plans.

- Our ground crew, who kept our old B-24 in perfect shape.

- All combat crewmen who flew these covert missions with me. Each member contributed greatly to our success.

- The 801st/492nd Bombardment Group Association. Our Maverick Group was part of the Eighth Air Force in England during World War II; however, our covert combat orders came from the Office of Strategic Services in London. It took great effort over several postwar years by the officers of our Veterans' Association that our group was officially designated as the 801st/492nd Bombardment Group in "The Mighty Eighth."

I especially wish to thank Sebastian H. Corriere, president; Richard T. Sizemore, vice president; I. Pete Petrenko, secretary/treasurer; and Frank E. Ostrow, director.

The officers of the 801st/492nd Bombardment Group Association designed the above logo that became official in 1994.

Most Americans are not aware of the "Carpetbaggers" of World War II. The following figures reveal the important contributions of this secret group to the defeat of Hitler. The author expresses sincere gratitude to the officers of the Carpetbagger Veterans Association for their permission to include these statistics in this book.

A BLACK B-24 LIBERATOR BOMBER TAKING OFF FROM U.S. AIR FORCE STATION #179 AT HARRINGTON, ENGLAND DURING WORLD WAR II. CLANDESTINE NIGHT MISSIONS WERE FLOWN FROM THIS SECRET BASE. DROPPING MUNITIONS AND SUPPLIES TO UNDERGROUND RESISTANCE FORCES IN NAZI OCCUPIED EUROPE. FROM APRIL 5, 1944, TO APRIL 27, 1945. THE 801/492ND BOMB GROUP "CARPET-BAGGERS" ALSO PARACHUTED AGENTS INTO FRANCE, HOLLAND, NORWAY, DEN-MARK AND GERMANY FOR SPYING AND ESPIONAGE ACTIVITIES, IN ADDITION TO FLYING NIGHT BOMBING MISSIONS.

| B-24 AIRCRAFT COMPLEMENT | 69 | NUMBER OF SORTIES | 3,000 |
|---|---|---|---|
| AIRCRAFT MISSING IN ACTION | 26 | OSS AGENTS DROPPED | 556 |
| AIRCREW KILLED IN ACTION | 197 | TONNAGE TO UNDERGROUND | 4,511 |
| AIRCREW KILLED IN TRAINING | 11 | NIGHT BOMBING MISSIONS | 21 |

# FOREWORD
## by William E. Colby

Older men start—and run—wars, but young men fight them. At no time was this more true than in World War II, started and directed by Adolph Hitler and resisted by Winston Churchill, Franklin Roosevelt and Joseph Stalin, who all had their roots in the World War I generation. But the fighting was done, as it was over the centuries, by the young men.

Dr. Fesmire has written a warm and inspiring account of how one young man responded to his country's call in World War II. It reflects how that war reached an entire generation of American youths in their small towns throughout the U.S., trained them in complex and novel techniques and sent them around the world to fight for freedom. In his case, that involved learning to fly huge four-motored bombers and guide them over hostile territory where other young men pointed antiaircraft weapons at them.

Dr. Fesmire's amusing accounts of some of his mishaps and adventures in training inspire similar memories in his readers who went through such experiences. But when he gets to his specific role during the war, he opens a page of history which has received almost no attention in the post-War world.

The reason is that this work by Dr. Fesmire was necessarily held in the deepest of secrecy at the time, so few records or "war stories" about it came to public attention thereafter. But some of us who were dependent on that work know full well its importance, and are glad to see it included in the history of that time through Dr. Fesmire's book.

Because it made a major contribution to the Allied success during the War, and to the revival of Europe's free nations after the war. Dr. Fesmire's flights over enemy held country—in the dark of night in black painted aircraft—were to bring secret operators, weapons and equipment to the resistance forces of the occupied nations so they could strike the enemy from the rear while the allied armies struck them from the front. They may not have defeated the enemy in pitched battles, but the fact that they were everywhere in the occupied territories forced the enemy to use masses of troops and weapons to guard against them, troops who were consequently not available to use against the allied armies.

As one of those who flew with Dr. Fesmire—half the trip, as I parachuted out to my own mission—I know the difficulties and dangers Dr. Fesmire faced in navigating in the dark looking for little bonfires lit by reception committees of the local resistance forces, who were avidly hoping for the arrival of the stocks of explosives and the men he was carrying. My own mission into the mountains of North Norway required Dr. Fesmire to dodge among the mountain tops (which one of his colleagues hit on a later effort to resupply us, killing all aboard) and keep a sharp eye on his fuel consumption as the target was at the far limits of his possible range. And yes, we did have to dig out one of his tires which sank into a soft airfield in Northern Scotland from which we took off.

Dr. Fesmire and I didn't know each other then, as security discipline required that the air crews only be told where to drop their passengers and cargo, not their identities, nationalities or missions. The fear was that they might be shot down and captured on some later mission and placed under pressure by the enemy to tell all they knew. If they did not know, they could not tell. It was only long after the War that Dr. Fesmire and I made contact despite our close cooperation for a few hours over Norway.

But mine was only one mission, and Dr. Fesmire and his fellow "Carpetbaggers" as they came to be called ranged throughout occupied Europe on repeated trips. These young Americans from the small towns, farms and cities of America were a key element of the massive war machine our country built out of almost nothing from 1941 to 1945. Dr. Fesmire's account of his experience, aside from the facts of what he did, shows the values, the courage and the will which united the nation at that time in a great cause. It proves also that those qualities are still in our free society—they only need to be aroused and mobilized for the other challenges our nation faces now and in the future.

# Table of Contents

# INTRODUCTION

World War II was the most destructive war in human history in terms of lives and property, yet Hollywood still was able to romanticize many of the battles, such as the Normandy invasion and the Battle of the Bulge. Any veteran knows that such battles were far from glamorous, and that the war was won by ordinary men doing their jobs, and doing them well.

There is a part of the war of which most Americans are not aware. An important, secret war was waged by the Office of Strategic Services (OSS, the forerunner of the CIA) and underground resistance fighters against the German troops in Nazi-occupied countries. The men and women of these forces were just as vital to the war effort as the infantry was. The underground agents not only sabotaged key German military installations and killed enemy soldiers, they also transmitted important military information to the Allied Command. A consistent supply of reliable intelligence proved to be a major stumbling block for Adolf Hitler in his quest for world domination.

I was a part of this secret war. At age of twenty-one I became a pilot for a crew of Carpetbaggers, whose mission it was to make night flights over occupied countries and drop OSS men and supplies to the underground. At the time all I knew was that I belonged to a division of the 856th Squadron of the 801st/492nd Bomb Group. Our efforts were so secret that the code name "Carpetbaggers" was not released until after the war.

As a whole, the Carpetbaggers made thousands of drops. We received limited training for these covert missions, but the excellent intelligence supplied by OSS almost made up for it. The underground communicated the strength and positions of German antiaircraft guns to London on a daily basis, and our intelligence officer used this information to draw up a flight plan that kept us clear of enemy guns.

I said that the intelligence almost made up for the lack of training we received. There were situations for which we were not trained, such as the time we expected no enemy shelling but found ourselves in the middle of it. Or the mission to Norway where we dropped Major William Colby and his OSS team. Or the time a well known and well-respected colonel gave us a flight plan that almost caused us to crash. Or the time our plane was hit while we were behind enemy lines.

I was used to using my own judgment ever since I had been a child, and the experience carried over into my military life. I became a maverick pilot, and it contributed to our crew's becoming one of the few to complete all of the missions we attempted. Some pilots aborted at least a few of their missions, because of bad weather. There were at least two Carpetbagger crews I knew who were killed during their missions, resulting in the loss of about twenty-five lives. I heard stories about other losses, but I didn't know the people involved.

I know that I can safely speak for all the Carpetbaggers when I say that they are proud of their records and their contributions to this secret war. It is not my intention to present a historic study of the Carpetbaggers. Let's leave that to the historians. Instead, what I offer are true stories of my experiences, most of them told from the vantage point of a Carpetbagger pilot—the window of a black B-24.

Robert H. Fesmire
February, 1995

# 1

# Becoming a Maverick

The numerous experiences during the early years of my life contributed greatly to my success and survival as a Carpetbagger pilot in the secret war against Hitler.

I was born near Lexington, Tennessee on May 6, 1923, the third of 6 children born to Reverend W. J. Fesmire, a Methodist minister, and Eula Fesmire. Although it sounds like a cliché, I'm convinced that no one could have had better parents. Even though all of us grew up during the Depression years, we were happy as a family. They taught us to focus on the important things in life, such as family, good grades in school, and friendships. Since no one else had many material possessions, it was easy for my parents to show us how relatively unimportant they were.

It was important for us to learn discipline early on, because a family had to live as a team to survive. My first taste of discipline came to me in the form of chores. I had to help milk the cows, mow the yard, wash, feed the chickens, whatever had to be done. I enjoyed most of my chores, but detested weeding the garden.

Between the ages of twelve and fifteen, as a newspaper delivery boy for the *Nashville Banner* and *Nashville Tennessean*, I made enough money during these years to buy my own clothes, a bicycle, and pleasure spending. Keeping a schedule of early morning and late afternoon deliveries of newspapers helped prepare me for military discipline.

Being preacher's kids and knowing about discipline didn't mean we were little angels. We just had to be extra careful not to damage the image of a preacher's family. Occasionally we would mess up windows on Halloween, steal fruit from a neighbor's orchard, or swipe a watermelon from a nearby farmer. (I got caught doing this only once, but the farmer never told my parents.)

I always made good grades in school, and I'm afraid I owe at least some of that accomplishment to a bit of larceny I committed when I was 12. It was summer, school was out, and I had nothing to occupy my mind. There was no TV as there is today. There was an old radio, but it only worked part of the time. Nor was there a library, until I made one of my own. I found a window in the grammar school, opened it, and took out three or four books at a time. When I finished reading them, I would go back and exchange the ones I'd read for three or four new ones. In that manner I read most of the books in the library. I really didn't consider it a crime, since I always brought the books back. No loss, and my gain.

Sometimes I'd get bored, and simply wander off in search of adventure. Once, when I was twelve, a friend of mine and I decided that we wanted to hike to the Cumberland River and spend a few days. My parents trusted me, but they had no idea when we'd come back.

During my pre-teen years I had many other experiences that taught me how to survive a crisis. I spent a lot of time with my older brother, Fleetwood, and his friends, who had adopted me as their mascot. They spent a lot of their time doing things that were probably not safe for them, and definitely not safe for a twelve-year-old. It's not that they dared me to do the same things they did; they simply expected me to.

I was about eight or nine when they swam across a flooded river. They were strong enough to go straight across, but when my turn came, I found myself in a strong cross current, and it was sweeping me farther and farther downstream. Fleetwood and his friends ran along the bank and shouted out encouragement as I struggled toward them. I made it, and even though I wound up a hundred yards downstream from where I started. I discovered that I wasn't afraid of anything, although I should have been. One of Fleetwood's classmates drowned later that same year when he tried to swim the river from the same spot I had.

Another time Fleetwood, his friends, and I were on one of our watermelon gathering trips. We were in the middle of the patch when we heard two shotgun blasts. The older boys ran like rabbits and jumped across the fence before I even realized that I was alone. I knew I couldn't outrun an adult, so I dived into some high weeds close by, and for the first time in my life I was happy to see weeds. I lay still for about 5 minutes, listening carefully and hardly daring to breathe.

When I felt the coast was clear, I jumped up and ran toward my brother and his friends. They were about half a mile a way, hidden in some woods. They asked if I was okay. I said I was, and I appreciated their concern. I also knew that not one of them (Fleetwood excepted) would go back and check on me, because the man with the shotgun was probably still around.

I thought Fleetwood was the greatest older brother anyone could have, and the fact that his friends accepted me brought us even closer together. He wasn't one to pick a fight, but anyone who took him on always lost.

The bishop had the authority to move a Methodist pastor at any time to serve a church in another town, and each new move meant that we would have to work to become accepted in a strange place. Most of the time the bishop made good decisions, but a few times we children thought the bishop was stupid. Our father was a true Christian in serving God. He always obeyed the bishop's orders with respect and dignity.

During four years Dad was a District Superintendent over approximately twenty-five pastors. The pastors showed their respect for Dad by electing him as one of the five hundred worldwide ministers as delegates to the United Methodist Conference. The purpose was to unite all the branches that had separated during the Civil War.

My wonderful mother was four feet and ten inches tall, and it was obvious she was head of the household. She was a perfect help-mate for my father. She always strived that my father and we six children be winners. My parents stressed God, family, and country, and they were very proud that all four sons served in the military.

As a teenager, I made one of the most important decisions in my life. My dad was a pastor at the Methodist Church in Baxter, and I was a high school student at Baxter Seminary, a Methodist prep school. It was an excellent school, and no sooner had I gotten used to it when the bishop transferred my dad to another town. I had no desire to leave my school and was determined to graduate from Baxter.

Dr. Upperman, the president of Baxter Seminary, offered me the opportunity to live in the dormitory and work my way through school. When I relayed Dr. Upperman's suggestion to my parents, they agreed. They were pleased that I had the chance to advance my education in this way. Thus I was weaned from my family at an early age, but the work I had to do at the school left little time to miss them. My studies, twenty-eight hours of work per week, and extracurricular activities kept me busy.

I had several jobs at Baxter Seminary. Some of them included firing our dormitory coal furnace, carpentry, pouring concrete, laying bricks, painting, and other sundry odd jobs. The one that took the most self-discipline was getting up at 4:30 on a cold winter morning to milk cows. I was also on the football and track teams, and during my last two years in high school, I was a state reporter for *The Nashville Tennessean* newspaper. I earned a few dollars each month for reporting school and local news.[1]

What little free time we had was structured and supervised. We could date, but we couldn't leave the campus. We, along with our chaperons, would sit on the grass and talk, or go square dancing in the girl's dormitory. Kissing a girl was out of the question; holding her hand was about as intimate as we could get. I know. I found out the hard way.

There was an attractive girl who lived in the girl's dormitory. I asked if it would be okay to take her to church on Sunday evening, and the chaperon said it would. On the way, I couldn't help noticing how pretty my date looked. Finally I couldn't resist. It was dark, and I figured the chaperon couldn't see me. I slipped my arm around her waist. My bold action earned a smile from my date and a whack on the back with a rod by our chaperon.

A major event took place in 1941, a few weeks before my high school graduation. Congressman Albert Gore, Sr., came to our school that spring to address the student body. We were acutely aware of the war against Hitler and were concerned that the United States would become involved. We were also afraid of what Japan might do.

---

1  My news was mailed to Russell Finney, Sate Editor of the *Tennessean*. My military records include letters of recommendations to the Army Air Corps that had been written during World War II by Silliman Evans, President, and Coleman Harwell, Executive Director of the *Tennessean*.

Congressman Gore gave a splendid speech on international issues. He talked about the war in Europe and assured us that our country would not be actively involved. At the end of his speech he answered questions. Rupurt Nunally's question always made an impression on me, and I never forgot the answer.

"Congressman Gore," he asked, "our country is selling a lot of scrap iron to Japan. They're building battleships with it. Will that create a danger for us?"

Gore stuck his chest out, smiled smugly, and replied. "America doesn't have to worry about Japan. If they started a war, we could destroy that island country in two weeks."

His reply brought a rousing cheer and made us proud to be Americans. Of course Congressman Gore, other leaders in Washington, and the rest of America suffered a rude awakening when Japan attacked Pearl Harbor later that winter.

I graduated valedictorian of my class at Baxter Seminary. Dr. and Mrs. Harry Upperman, headmasters of the school, had great influence on my life. Their religious influence, combined with my work and studies, contributed greatly to a happy and meaningful life for me, as well as for the other students who attended the school. Some of them had had problems with the law, but at Baxter they were kept too busy to get in trouble. I shall always remember Baxter Seminary's motto: Truth, Honor, Loyalty, Service.

My parents showed pride and encouragement when I entered Vanderbilt in the fall of 1941 and began a major in chemical engineering. The quality of education offered at Baxter was so high that most of my freshman courses were a review of my high school studies. While at college, I continued to work at odd jobs, though Fleetwood and my parents helped supplement my income. After the Japs bombed Pearl Harbor, most of us went to school throughout year-round. On this accelerated program I finished two years of engineering in March, 1943.

By the fall of 1941, students were aware of the war in Europe; however, we weren't seriously concerned. Our major source of heartburn came from a student named Latimer. He never went anywhere without his copy of Hitler's autobiography, Mein Kampf, and he challenged other students to listen to him explain why Germany should win the war against France and England. He told us about his Germanic ancestry, and of some relatives still living there. He preached Hitler's concept of the master race, and he actively tried to win students over to his version of the Nazi Party. He approached me once, but I refused to listen to his radical beliefs. He was crazy.

After December 7th, Latimer could no longer be ignored. One day shortly after the Japanese attack, Latimer was preaching his usual Nazi gospel when a group of students listening to him decided that they'd heard enough. Some of them seized him, while the others pulled the book away from him. They tore Mein Kampf into shreds, then proceeded to beat Latimer. He never tried to convert another student, and we considered what we did to him a small victory. But it could not help us overcome the feeling of shock brought about by Pearl Harbor, for we realized for the first time that we could be inducted into service at a moment's notice.

Many of my classmates volunteered within weeks of the attack. I figured it was just a matter of time before I was drafted, and I knew I didn't want to fight on the ground. Gradually, I became eager to be inducted into the military, and in early December, 1942, I made the decision that I wanted to become a pilot. After taking tests and a medical exam, I was sworn into the Army Air Corps reserves on December 12, 1942. I was able to stay in school until the following March.

I was eager for active duty. I had completed all math and science courses. My good grades, including top marks in math, gave me great confidence that I would be successful in becoming a pilot.

# 2

# The Road to My Commission

Several classmates and I received orders for active duty in the Army Air Corps. We were to be stationed at Kessler field in Biloxi, Mississippi for basic training. Most of us were eager to be activated, and we hoped to be trained as pilots. We were to report in early April of 1943.

A crowd of us college students and their concerned parents congregated at Nashville's Union Station during the late afternoon on the first Sunday in April. We were allowed a small traveling bag to pack a few possessions. A sergeant did a roll call as we lined up to go aboard the L&N troop train. When my name was called, I looked at my parents briefly. Their faces showed no emotion, but I knew that this was for my benefit. They wanted me to concern myself with doing my job and not worrying about them. I also knew that they were used to moving at the whim of a bishop, and that they understood the importance of honoring one's duty. I smiled at them, then boarded the train.

We arrived early Monday morning. A sergeant came rushing down the aisle shouting, "You're in the Army now! Depart from the train and get in formation. You are at Kessler Field Army Air Corps Base, and we're gonna make soldiers out of all you sad sacks!"

We did as he said. After another roll call, we were herded toward the uniform and equipment issue building. When I had changed I took my civilian clothes and stuffed them into the trash.

Basic training at Kessler Field would be my greatest hurdle in becoming an officer and pilot. My life had been different from most young men. School and work had kept me too busy to become involved with cigarettes or alcohol. But I was around my share of beautiful girls during my teenage years, and I felt sexually attracted to some of them. In spite of my best efforts, though, I remained a virgin. My religious environment had a great influence on my life.

I knew basic training would be hell, but I had self-discipline. I became a maverick in anticipating problems, and I did my best in reaching my goal of earning my pilot's wings. My net pay for the six weeks at Kessler was $38—the most money I had ever had at one time—and I earned every cent.

I had known several of the fellows in our group from school days. Bob Grace, a classmate at Baxter Seminary, and Al Fehrman from Vanderbilt had been close friends for many years.[2] We spent several days with physical exams, written exams, and shot after shot after shot in our arms. On the second

---

2  The two friends earned their wings and commissions. They were pilots in the 8th Air Force in England. They survived the war; however, Fehrman was a prisoner of War after his plane was shot down by the Germans. Both men had successful postwar careers.

day we began marching and drilling in military formations. Many of the fellows in our group were unruly from the beginning. Our master sergeant compared us to wild horses that had to be broken.

The first crisis I had at Kessler occurred during an Articles of War film, which covered the legal rights and duties of a soldier. About all that I remembered of that film was that military law was strict. We had just received our last shots, and I was feeling very dizzy and ready to faint. I knew that if I passed out in front of the sergeant I could end up in the hospital and wash out of training for medical reasons. I didn't want this to happen. So when they began to show the film, I staggered outside, crawled under the building, and passed out. I was lucky. No one saw me, even though it was mid-afternoon.

I woke up about thirty minutes later and felt much better. My luck still held. No one noticed when I walked back into the darkened room in time to see the last few minutes of the film. Fortunately, we had no exam.

Several kitchen police duties and one latrine duty were nightmares enough for me. These duties were generally the punishment of all for the misbehavior of a few. We had a short master sergeant who was about 35 years old. He acted pretty tough and claimed he was a lawyer in civilian life. He enjoyed screaming at us, and we thought he was the biggest jerk ever to wear a uniform. I didn't know it then, but I'd eventually meet a few officers who were much worse.

A few days after arriving at Kessler Field, several of us were milling around and goofing off on the grounds around the barracks, when up came the master sergeant. He put his hands on the heads of a couple of men.

Come with me, gentlemen, " he said. "The two of you have latrine duty."

The men he picked broke loose and ran into our crowd. The whole group started running around in circles, the sergeant yelling and trying to grab someone all the while. Eventually he solved the problem by putting all of us on KP.

This wasn't the first time I pulled KP at Kessler. During one tour I lost quite a bit of weight while operating a device nicknamed the Chinese Clipper. It was a large metal compartment through which food trays were run for steam cleaning. The steam poured from the Clipper into the room, and it must have been at least 130 degrees. I sweated so much I must have lost 10 pounds.

Another KP tour of duty lasted from 6 pm to 6 am. It wasn't too bad, but the following results were disastrous. When we got off duty the next morning we were ordered to get in line outside the mess hall for breakfast before returning to the barracks. Beautiful roses, bordered by a low picket fence, were growing outside the mess hall. We were exhausted after 12 straight hours of duty, and some of us were sitting on the fence. An officer came out of the kitchen and saw us.

"You GI's get off the fence and get in line!" he shouted. "Blow it out your ass!" someone close to me yelled back. I flinched, but the officer didn't seem to notice.

When we entered the mess hall, a lieutenant standing by the door said, "I know you soldiers are tired from all-night KP. Go to that far end of the room and stay together. We'll give you a good breakfast with special service."

We thought we had struck lucky, but we were wrong. After eating this special breakfast, we were ordered back into the kitchen for 12 more hours of KP!

It didn't take long for me to come up with a way to get out of KP. Military policy forbids a GI to work in the kitchen if he has an open lesion on either hand. Their reasoning was that the food could become contaminated and cause the GI's (diarrhea). So I kept a minor open cut on my right thumb, and I didn't let it heal until my KP days were history. To this day I still have a battle scar on my thumb. I still think I should have gotten a Purple

Heart for it. After all, I was wounded in the line of duty, or to avoid duty.

The precision of a military group marching in formation is truly a beautiful and fantastic sight. Their steps and head movements are synchronized because they bounce on their feet when they walk. In fact, most people have an up-and-down head movement while walking or marching.

I don't.

As a teenager, I enjoyed hunting game. I had learned to glide my steps in sneaking up on game in order to get a good shot Without realizing it, this stride became my normal way of walking, and it goes without saying that an officer had no trouble picking me out of a formation. So because I interfered with the elegance of our squadron's marching, I was ordered to clean commodes, wash basins, floors, showers, and walls in the latrines.

I finally decided to discuss my problem with our drill sergeant.

"Sarge," I said, "you know why I've been punished?"

"Sure do," he replied in a Mississippi drawl.

"I don't think it's fair. After all, it's how I walk every day of my life. And I just don't think I should be punished for that."

"Neither do I," he replied. "But look, next time we march, get into the middle of the formation. The lieutenant will never notice you."

I did as he said, and true to his word, I never cleaned another toilet in the military again. Now I understood why everyone loved this drill sergeant.

I saw the ocean for the first time in my life when we were drilled on the beaches on the Gulf of Mexico. It was the only place where we could all train, and hundreds of us had marching drills on the sandy beach. Sometimes the wind would gust and kick up so much dust and sand that we could hardly see anyone within a hundred yards. The dust also caused respiratory problems for most of us, and many of our group washed out because of it. It gave me some trouble, but I was determined to fly, and I kept quiet.

Judgment day finally came after six weeks of basic training. Many of our group washed out, and their dreams of becoming pilots were crushed. All of my close friends and I were successful in clearing this first hurdle. When I later flew combat missions, I thought how much easier they were than the battles I fought at Kessler Field. The hell I went through there was worth it, because it prepared me for combat.

## College Training Detachment

My next assignment was a pleasant surprise. All of us who were successful in basic training were stationed at colleges or universities for the equivalent of freshmen year studies in science and math. Many pre-cadets in our group had little or no schooling after high school graduation, and they needed more education to become pilots. I was transferred to Cookeville, Tennessee to study at the College Training Detachment at Tennessee Tech.

Most of our group spent five months at Tennessee Tech to qualify for cadet training. As a student at Vanderbilt I had already completed much more than required. I had only to complete ten hours of pilot training in a Piper Cub.

I had never been in a plane before; in fact, I had driven less than ten hours in an automobile. As I made my first takeoff, I found that I loved flying as much as I had ever loved the idea of flying.

The pilot instructor expressed favorable comments on my performance. After completing the required ten hours, I was shocked by a comment he made. He said that he doubted I could make it as a pilot. Of course, I did not agree with his opinion, and I became determined to prove him wrong.

It was a pleasant surprise to be stationed at Cookeville, since Baxter Seminary was only eight miles away. Being so close to my home grounds, I began to reminisce about my alma mater. I also had the chance to go out and visit the town.

One day, without a pass, a buddy and I were walking down a street when we saw a large, heavy set man in civilian clothes driving his car up to us, got out, and called to us.

"You soldiers come here!"

We immediately recognized him as Dr. Everett Derryberry, the president of Tennessee Tech. We knew he would report us, but only if he could catch us. We sprinted away, and he began to run after us. Many years earlier Dr. Derryberry was on the football team while a student at the University of Tennessee. He made a good try, but now he was too fat and we were too fit for there to be much of a contest. We ducked around a corner and took a couple of side streets before sneaking back to the campus. We were scared that he had recognized us and that we'd get in trouble, but nothing came of the incident.

My six weeks at Tennessee Tech passed quickly, and soon I was ready for a transfer to the Classification Center in Nashville to complete the next step in becoming a pilot.

## Classification Center in Nashville

During June, 1943, the Classification Center tested us in every way to determine if we were qualified for pilot, navigator, or bombardier training. I found out about my first test by reading a notice on the bulletin board. Someone had seen fit to put me in a group to do KP.

After all the KP duty I pulled during basic training, I wasn't about to spend another hour with the Chinese Clipper. With the help of a pocket knife, I created the same excuse that had worked so well at Kessler Field. It worked again, and there was no more KP duty for me. Higher command may have thought that details of punishment would give us combat discipline, but I'd had enough.

We underwent a fantastic number of tests at the Classification Center. We had to be in excellent physical condition and have an excellent mental aptitude. There were several written tests. We were tested in a chamber depressurized to the equivalent of 15,000 to 20,000 feet to see if sinus or ear problems would interfere with high altitude operations. And we were tested in a pitch-black chamber for night vision. The dim image of a question was on the screen in front of us, and we had to scratch out the answer on a sheet of paper. I had the highest possible grade in night vision, and later would have vivid memories of this test later during my night combat missions.

But the most unusual test I had was an examination by a military psychologist. He asked me general questions about my family background ("What was your childhood like?"), education ("Exactly what did you study at Vanderbilt?"), religion ("Do you attend church regularly?"), my social life ("Do you have a girlfriend?"), and so on.

I calmly answered each of his questions, no matter how silly or trivial they seemed to me. Then the major turned to the subject of sex.

"Did you ever have sex with your mother or sister?"

I was amazed and shocked by the incredulity of the question; nevertheless, I calmly answered "No, Sir".

Finally the major was finished with his questions. After friendly conversation he assured me that I would be approved for pilot training.

"Just one more thing, Sir," I asked. The major nodded for me to continue.

"Sir, I really want to be a pilot. I'll be a good pilot. But if they decide that my math background can be put to better use as a navigator, then I'll be the best one in the Corps. But I'd appreciate whatever you can do to make sure I get to be a pilot."

The major assured me that he would forward my request, then he dismissed me. I was glad the interview was over, and thought it a hell of a way to earn my pilot's wings. I saluted and left.

Two days later we were ready to leave the Classification Center. An hour before we found out what we would be doing for the rest of the war, I was called out of line and told to report to one of the majors in the office. I walked to his office, entered, and saluted.

"Fesmire, the staff psychologist tells me that you are willing to be either a navigator or a pilot."

"Yes, Sir, that's correct," I answered.

"Well, I want to know which one you want to be."

"Sir, I would love to be a pilot. The only reason I volunteered my services as a navigator was because, considering my education, I figured it would be easy. But I really want to be a pilot, Sir."

He picked up a sheet of paper and scratched something out.

"You were approved for both assignments, and I've just erased your navigator designation. You'll be a pilot, if that's really what you want."

"Yes, Sir, it is. Thank you, Sir."

I was still a cadet when I walked out of his office, but in my mind I was already a pilot.

My monthly net pay would become $75—quite a lot of money in 1943. I left Nashville two months later to begin cadet preflight school at Maxwell Field in Montgomery, Alabama. I had changed during the past several months. I had cleared the unpleasant hurdles in becoming an aviation cadet, and I was confident I would become a pilot.

## Maxwell Field

I arrived at Maxwell Field in the summer of 1943. Our preflight education included math, weather, Morse code, navigation, and aircraft and ship identification. I found classwork easy, since I had a good college background, but some of the other men in our group who had just completed high school had to struggle.

There was also a lot of physical training, since it was essential that we remain physically and mentally ready for the rigors of combat flight. Our training also dictated a strict dress code. Our uniforms had to be neat, and we had to be clean shaven with a short hair cut. We had to stand straight, sit straight, and keep our eyes straight forward.

We had to keep our barracks clean and neat. Each morning at reveille we had to put our bunks in perfect order. The mattresses, blankets, sheets, and pillow cases were folded and stacked neatly at the end of the bunk.

Since there were no chairs in the barracks, the only place to sit was on the exposed half of the bunk's metal springs—if we got the chance to sit at all. But it happened that one Sunday morning we had some free time. The cadet next to me was a small man, but since we all took showers together, we couldn't help but see that at least one portion of this man's anatomy was definitely not proportional to his stature. Therefore, we gave him the flattering nickname, Tripod. No one paid much attention when Tripod came back from his shower and sat down on the springs of his bunk. And he was totally unaware (for the moment, anyway) that his weight had compressed the springs, making them wider, therefore allowing his testicles to slip through the rings.

He realized he was trapped when he tried to stand up.

"YEEEEEEEOOOOOOOOOOWWWWWWW!"

We turned and saw Tripod doubled over in agony, his testicles caught between the springs. As his predicament dawned on us, we began to laugh. Then we saw he was in serious trouble. As long as he sat still he was okay. But whenever he tried to stand up, the springs tightened around his balls, and his voice would rise another octave.

"Hey, fellas, come on," he finally pleaded. "Help me out!"

We thought about the problem until a man slid under Tripod's bunk and pulled the springs down to enlarge the opening. It was hard not to laugh at Tripod while trapped like this. It was even harder not to laugh at his rescuer, with his face inches from Tripod's bottom. At last Tripod was free, and he stood up to our loud cheers and whistles.

Two other events that happened while I was at Maxwell weren't as funny. I was sound asleep one night when I heard someone scream "Gas! Gas!" I sat up at once and saw a dense haze that filled the room. The odor from it was repulsive, and I quickly learned its source. A masked man in a sergeant's uniform was spraying it through the barracks. I immediately grabbed my gas mask and thrust my face into it, then ran out of the room to the fresh air outside. We waited there until the tear gas had cleared from our quarters, then marched back in to catch what few hours of sleep were left.

Another time we were awakened at midnight by our sergeant, though he had no gas this time.

"This is a drum-out, men!" our sergeant called. "Get your best uniform on and get into formation outside. Move it!"

We had no idea what a drum-out was, but the drums outside beating a steady, solemn rhythm gave us the impression it was a very serious thing. I was especially impressed when outside I saw the entire company of cadets at Maxwell standing in perfect formation.

When we were all accounted for, a voice came over the public address system.

"Cadets, we have called you out tonight to remind you that you are expected to conduct yourself as gentlemen at all times.. Gentlemen are always honest. Unfortunately, I have the sad duty to inform you that some of you have disgraced the military by cheating on exams. After I read these names of those guilty, none of you will ever mention them again on this base. If you do, you will be washed out immediately."

The names thundered out over the speakers, and as I listened to them, I wondered why they would be so stupid to risk being washed out. Everyone knew the rules when they came here, and everyone had to have excellent references just to get this far.

Now these men probably would be privates for the rest of their military service.

The voice dismissed us, and we returned to our quarters. It was too bad for the men who had been expelled, but the example worked. That was the only drum-out I ever had to attend.

Looking back, it was amazing how little we knew about what was going on in Europe and in the Pacific. We were busy constantly, and we didn't have the time to reflect on the big picture of World War II. Our thoughts were centered on learning how to accomplish our mission, and to come out alive.

## Primary Flight Training

During October in 1943, I arrived at Douglas, Georgia for about six weeks of primary flight training in a Stearman PT-17 plane. The Stearman looked like an antique bi-winged plane, and there was no radio in it. The primary airfield was just as primitive. Planes took off and landed on grass.

After several days of ground school, we began our flight training. Mr. Harley B. Pickett, Jr. was my flight instructor, and we hit it off perfectly. He was a great person, and I learned to love him. I took him to be somewhere in his forties, and since he was a civilian pilot, I guessed that something had kept him out of military service. And because he wasn't military, he was easier to get along with

I soloed after ten hours of flying with him. I was nervous during the flight, and I confess that it wasn't my best. I bounced a few times during my landing, and I felt more foolish with each bounce. Finally the plane stopped. Thoroughly embarrassed, I taxied over to where Mr. Pickett stood.

"Okay, that was a little rough, but don't worry about it," he told me. "Take the plane up again. Just relax and you'll do fine."

I taxied around again and took off. This time I was calmer, and I enjoyed it more. The flight was smoother, and I made a perfect landing.

"Told you you'd do better the next time," he said when I had taxied over to him. "Now do that one more time."

I flew a third solo, and my performance was flawless. When I got down, Mr. Pickett nodded in approval.

"Okay, you're ready to go on your own," he told me. I was thrilled with both his praise and my accomplishment.

About a week later I was doing touch-and-go landing practice on an auxiliary field when I almost crashed. I had made a good landing but had delayed too long in hitting the throttle for a takeoff. The PT-17 slowly became airborne, but not fast enough for me, for large pine trees loomed ahead. I pulled back on the stick, but that just made the plane go slower. Then I remembered that I had to advance the throttle in order to avoid stalling out. I gave it all the throttle I could and made it over the trees, but I knew I had clipped a limb. I was lucky that it wasn't a crash.

I returned to the base airfield and made a good landing. I jumped out of the cockpit to find a pine limb stuck in the right wheel. I grabbed the evidence and hid it quickly. The good fortune I had enjoyed as a child apparently had not abandoned me; once again I was lucky to be alive, and once again no one could fuss at me because no one had seen what had happened.

A few days later I reported to the operation office to practice acrobatic flying with Mr. Pickett. The flight would be fun, and the weather cooperated beautifully. I was waiting for Mr. Pickett to take me up when a second lieutenant I had never seen before approached me. He looked as though he was my age, and his face was angry.

"Mister!" he shouted to me. "What's your name?"

I told him.

"I'm going to take you up for a test flight. I just arrived at this base, and you're the first cadet I'm going to wash out." The hell you are, I thought to myself even as I clamped my teeth together. I had learned in basic that talking back to an officer gets you nowhere fast.

21

The crazy lieutenant went on to explain that he had finished cadet training and was commissioned just a month ago. He had applied for fighter pilot training but wasn't accepted. The lieutenant didn't say exactly why he didn't make it, but I figured that they didn't need fighters now, and that perhaps he wouldn't make a good bomber pilot. He had been sent to this primary airfield as an instructor pilot. He wasn't happy about the assignment, and he was ready to sacrifice a few cadets here to make him feel better.

He was angry throughout my test flight. I was frustrated, but tried my best to impress him with my skill. As I began my landing, I began to think that he was bluffing about washing me out, that he was just trying to shake me up to see how I would react under pressure.

But he was serious. All he said as we left the plane was, "You're through as a cadet."

I was dumbfounded, but Mr. Pickett was livid when he heard the news.

"I'm going to the base commander and straighten out that young shave-tail!" he told me. And within an hour he was back with good news. The hot-shot lieutenant was ordered to give me another test flight during the following week, and that it would be successful.

Without letting anyone know, Mr. Pickett gave me two practice flights during the week. He was pleased with my skill in all maneuvers and assured me once again that I would pass the flight test. I couldn't have had a better friend, and I loved him.

The day came for the test flight with the dumb lieutenant pilot. Aside from telling me which maneuver to make, he said nothing. This time after we landed he simply said, "Okay" and walked away. I rushed to find Mr. Pickett to tell him the good news.

About ten days later I was ready for basic flight training. Unlike other bases where I had trained, I felt a little sad leaving

Douglas. I would miss Mr. Harley B. Pickett, Jr., and I felt like I was leaving a friend behind.

## Basic Flight Training

In early January, 1944, I arrived at Cochran Field in Macon, Georgia for basic flight training in the BT-9. The Stearman I flew in primary flying had a few basic instruments, but the BT-9 had modern night navigational equipment. We had limited school work in basic flying; the emphasis was hands-on experience with instructor pilots. My instructor at Cochran closely monitored my flight performance, and eventually told me it was excellent.

I thought I had learned to avoid trouble, but I had two close calls at Cochran. On one occasion I was guilty, but it was not intentional, and the commanding officers were not aware of this goof. On the second occasion, however, I was innocent, but it gave me a serious scare.

I hadn't been off base at any time during my first ten months of active duty in the Army Air Corps. A cadet friend and I decided to visit Macon on a Saturday night. We were supposed to be back at the base by 11 pm.

We felt pretty cocky fooling around the city. We were going to be commissioned pilots, and since it was our job to save the world, we were due some R&R during our intensive training. So my friend and I wound up in a bar where I drank the first and second beers of my life. The unstructured atmosphere of the bar (as well as the alcohol) made us relax more than we should have.

Suddenly I looked at my watch.

"Ohmygosh!" I cried. "It's nearly eleven!"

There was no doubt that we'd be late getting back to the base, so the question became how to avoid most of the trouble we knew was coming our way. I was rattled.

Fortunately a flight officer in our cadet class was in the bar with us. He had been an Army glider pilot, and was now taking regular pilot training at Cochran. He was an officer that didn't treat cadets like they were second-class citizens. The best thing about him that night was that he had a car, and that made him our savior.

"Listen, fellas," he told us. "Why don't you get into the trunk? I'll drive you through the gate and to your quarters. You can sneak in, and no one will ever know."

My friend and I looked at each other and quickly agreed. We crowded into the officer's trunk, and he drove to Cochran. No one stopped him on the way in, and he drove us right to our barracks. We climbed out of the trunk and rushed inside. Once I was in my bunk, I looked at my watch and saw that I was an hour late. But the officer was true to his word: no one ever found out about it, and this was the last foolish thing I did. As a cadet, anyway.

I was doing beautifully in basic flight training, and I was a happy 20-year-old kid. Within a few days I would move on to advanced flight training, but not before I got into serious trouble for something I did not do.

Six of us cadets shared one room in the barracks, and we became close friends. Around noon one day I walked into our room to find the rest of the guys sitting around my bunk gambling with dice. I had just sat down to watch when the dice rolled my way. I picked them up and tossed them back just in time for a captain to see me do it.

"Cadet, give me your name!" he barked. "You're in trouble!"

I felt a sinking feeling in my gut. I knew as well as anyone that gambling was forbidden by the cadet code, but I was not guilty of the crime. I also knew that to protest my innocence here would do no good. I gave the captain my name.

"Cadet Fesmire, I'll see to it that a hearing on this matter is set up with the board." He looked at me before he left. "looks like we're going to have to make an example out of you."

I was furious! Not only was I innocent, not one of my so-called friends spoke up for me.

My hearing was the next day. I was scared when I reported to it, but decided the best course of action would be to remain quiet and let the three board members do the talking. As a last resort, I could always tell the truth, though I doubted that another officer would take my word over that of a captain.

When I walked into the room, I immediately sensed fear. The captain who had set up the hearing and the other two officers there looked as though they felt uncomfortable with the entire process. Finally they got down to the business of going over my records, and I heard them murmur amazement at my high grades and excellent flight performance. At one point one of them suggested that I had too good a record to be washed out, and the others quickly agreed.

They finally addressed me for the first time during the hearing since they told me to sit down.

The problem, Cadet Fesmire," the senior officer said, "is the base colonel. He's been in a psychiatric hospital for a few months. Oh, he's out now, but, well, he's still crazy. Mean, too. I'm not exactly sure how he'd react to this hearing."

The officer stopped, and I could tell that they were all afraid of him. I suddenly noticed that the papers on the table were my official records. No one had written anything down.

The captain who had filed the charge against me spoke to his peers.

"Perhaps I overreacted to Cadet Fesmire's ... situation," he said. The other two nodded. Finally they agreed to give me a minor punishment of walking a three hour tour the following Saturday.

"I don't see any reason why any of us should discuss this matter outside this room," the senior officer observed. "Do you, cadet?"

"No, Sir."

Once again luck was with me. I assured the board officers that I would do my best in behavior and in cadet training. I saluted smartly and thanked them.

Saturday came, and I began my walking tour in front of the squadron headquarters. After about fifteen minutes I saw an officer approaching me. As he got closer I realized it was the same captain who had turned me in for throwing dice. He ordered me to stop for a moment.

"I just wanted to apologize for your punishment," he said. I didn't know what to say to that, so I settled for "Yes, Sir."

"In your case," he went on, "we were trying to follow military policy. Unfortunately, we have a colonel who is completely unpredictable. We have no idea what he would do to all of us if he found out about this incident. We're honestly in a damned-if-you-do-or-don't situation."

"I see, Sir," I replied, not exactly sure if I did or not. "Anyway, after I read your record, I realized that it would be a mistake to wash out such a fine and promising cadet as you. I'm telling you that I made an error in judgment about you, and I want you to understand that."

Does this guy realize how uncomfortable he's making me? I thought.

"Thank you, Sir," I answered. "No need to explain."

He nodded.

"Say, I just happened to think of something," he said after a moment. "My daughter will be visiting over the weekend. Would you like to come over to my house tonight and meet her?"

I was thoroughly frustrated now. I believed him when he said that my record impressed him, but I also suspected that another reason he wanted me to meet his daughter was to smooth over what had happened. I also thought it wrong for cadets to fraternize with officers. The whole thing felt wrong, and I just wanted to forget it as fast as I could.

"Sir, I thank you, but I just have to tell you that I don't know what to do."

After a pause he said, "Of course, I understand if you can't make it. But just remember that the colonel can get all of us in trouble. You remember not to say anything about the hearing?"

"Of course, Sir."

Suddenly, the captain excused me from my punishment, told me to go to my barracks, and to keep my mouth shut. With a salute and a smile, I thanked him. I had known good officers and bad officers throughout my year of active duty, and even though this captain had asked me to place myself in an awkward situation, I still respected him for admitting his mistake—especially to a cadet—and apologizing for it.

Otherwise, I was a happy cadet while completing basic flight training at Cochran Field. I was soon ready for advanced flight training, and I vowed to have no less than perfect behavior during my next assignment. I was determined to win my wings and commission as a lieutenant.

## Advanced Flight Training

During the middle of March, 1944, I was transferred to Columbus Air Force Base at Columbus, Mississippi for advanced training in a Beech craft AT-10, as well as for instrument training in a flight simulator. The AT-10 had twin engines.

The simulated flight instrument link trainer was a ground machine that had all of the instruments and controls of a real plane. It was even shaped like the front of a plane, but it had no windows. It had circular movements on a pivot, and the pilot was completely enclosed. The instructor might tell the student to take the fastest route from a heading of 90 degrees to 265 degrees. Students had to observe the instruments and fly accordingly.

I received much praise for my simulated instrument performance in the link trainer. After a few hours of flight instruction, I became skillful at flying the twin-engine AT-10. I had confidence in instrument flying and was comfortable with using the radio range.

One night, during a solo flight, something unusual happened. I was on approach for another routine landing, flaps down, and airspeed around 45 miles per hour. As the front two wheels made contact with the runway. I sensed the controls weren't responding. As I worked with them, the plane veered left as it rolled down the runway. The plane finally stopped before it ran off the pavement.

I found it wouldn't move when I tried to get off the runway. Just then a voice crackled over the radio. Another plane was making its final approach to land right behind me.

"Go around! Go around!" I screamed into the radio. "I'm parked on the runway!"

The incoming plane and the tower got the message in time. They aborted their landing and circled while a ground crew drove out to me. I awaited instructions in the cockpit while they inspected the plane. The left tire was flat, and they called for a tow. I rode back to operations in the jeep.

After two months in the advanced flight training program, I finally earned my wings and commission as a pilot. I got my request for a combat plane a 4-engine bomber.

On May 23, 1944, we had a very formal and meaningful graduation ceremony, during which we received our commissions and pilot's wings. My parents came all the way from Nashville to witness it. We were all thrilled over my accomplishments and laughed over the fact that I would be a pilot of a 4-engine bomber, despite having driven less than 20 hours in an automobile.

A few days after I received my wings I learned that Lieutenant Harry Sayles and a cadet were killed during a training mission the night after my graduation. Sayles had been a classmate in my engineering classes at Vanderbilt, and he was an outstanding college football player.

# 3

# B-24 Transition

The last time I was at Maxwell Field I was a lowly cadet.
Now, almost a year later, I was back as a commissioned pilot for
B-24 transitional training. What a difference in lifestyle a commission makes! I felt like I had come out of prison and become a
free man.

I was pleased to find that Dr. Thurman, my math professor at
Vanderbilt, was still at Maxwell. He was some ten or fifteen
years older than I was, and he had been inducted to teach math
to cadets. During ground school at Maxwell, a year earlier, I had
to call him Captain Thurman. Now that I was commissioned,
we were able to go into Montgomery occasionally for dinner.

One evening he and I were walking around the town search-
ing for a good restaurant, when suddenly a drunk private staggered up to us.

"Know what?" he said. "I'm gone beat the hell outta two officers!"

He began swinging at us, but we were able to dodge his swings and stay out of reach. I knew that even though we outranked and outnumbered him, the private had alcohol on his side, and that counted for more. This maverick decided to employ my philosophy on fighting: always avoid ones you can't win.

"Thurman," I said, "we don't want to be part of this. Can you run?"

"Sure."

"Come on, then!"

We must have made quite a sight, two officers sprinting down the sidewalk, and a drunk private chasing after and swinging at us all the way. I'm surprised that folks didn't think that Hitler might actually have a chance if this was the best our soldiers could do.

"There's a hotel up ahead," I shouted. "Let's lose him in there."

We ducked inside the lobby, and as I expected, the private didn't follow us in.

"Looks like we gave him the slip, Thurman."

I turned around in time to see my math professor slump down to the floor and pass out. Thurman rested against a wall for a few minutes, then announced that he felt better. Later I found out that he had a bad heart, and that the strain of running had almost killed him.

The B-24 was the largest aircraft I had ever flown, and the difference between it and the other airplanes I had flown was like the difference between a light truck and an 18-wheel trailer. Captain Gillis was my flight instructor throughout the three months of transitional training. With him in the copilot's seat I flew transition, navigation, bomb approach, formation, practice landings, night flights, and instrument flights. Once we went up to 30,000 feet. We wore oxygen masks, but mine malfunctioned, and I passed out. Gillis knew what to do, however. He quickly adjusted the valve that controlled my oxygen flow, and I woke up immediately. I was alert and felt just fine.

Captain Gillis was a skillful pilot and a great instructor. He was very friendly, and I enjoyed every flight with him. I also appreciated the fact that he shared his own experiences with me.

"When you go over there to England," he told me once, "remember that the weather will seldom cooperate with you when you land. Direct approaches from a mile out are dangerous in bad weather. So you need to learn how to make a low and tight approach."

Instead of flying high and parallel to the runway, then making a wide circular approach to it while descending, Gillis told me to stay parallel to the runway, but to get beneath the clouds and fly between 200-300 feet. Then, instead of the sweeping, wide approach, I should turn the plane nearly upside down and dive down to the runway. Gillis made me practice the landing maneuver until I felt comfortable with it, and I was glad he did. It came in handy over Norway.

It didn't take long for me to solo in the B-24. I enjoyed the flights when only a radio operator and flight engineer were aboard with me. I finally felt like a true pilot, and I owed a good deal of my confidence to Captain Gillis.

When we weren't on flight standby, we were free to go off the base. We went to the downtown bars, and I had my first drink of whiskey, followed by my second. I was young, I didn't know my limit, and I was soon drunk.

A few days later I was playing poker with some of the guys. We were drinking and gambling as night approached. I thought I knew my limit by this time, but I still got drunk. To make matters worse, I soon received an order to night solo within an hour. I had no choice but to show up for the flight.

I took off in the B-24 soon after dark, and without a copilot. I was doing well for fifteen minutes of flight, and by the time I was ready to land I thought surely the effects of the whiskey had worn off.

I had the plane on final approach, flaps down, wheels down, and the prop pitch was okay. I thought I was ready for the plane to touch down, and I throttled back. Suddenly the plane stalled and dropped straight down like a helicopter. The B-24 must have dropped 100 feet and there was a terrific jolt as the aircraft slammed onto the runway. It shook me up, but I wasn't hurt.

The control tower immediately called in an order for me to write up in the plane's log that the landing gear needed to be checked for damage. I complied with the order before getting out of the plane. A close inspection of the gear showed no damage, and I considered myself twice lucky. Neither the plane nor I suffered from my liquor landing.

Near the end of my transitional training I met a beautiful WAC at a mid-town bar. We hit it off perfectly, and I learned that she worked in an office across the street from my barracks. I took her to a movie at the base theater the following night. This practice was new to me; Baxter's academic and work requirements, like those of the military, were so strict that I had little spare time (to say nothing of spare money) to spend on dates. And while dating without a chaperon took a little getting used to, the fact that we liked each other very much soon made me forget about it, and we began to date every night.

Soon she revealed that she had had affairs with other pilots. She amazed me with her frankness and open aggressiveness; moreover, I couldn't understand why it didn't bother her.

"That's just the way I am, I guess," she replied. "It's like that every time."

"Every time?" I asked.

She smiled. "Every time a new group of pilots comes to the base, the same thing happens all over again. I always get involved with one of them. We have a wonderful relationship, and then he gets transferred out. Oh, they all say they'll write, but they never do, and I wind up hurt."

"So why do you keep getting involved?"

She looked at me. "I guess I'm just an incurable romantic at heart. You know what I mean?"

She smiled again, but there was more to it this time, and I was pretty sure that she wanted me. But I needed to be completely sure.

"I think so," I replied. "You mean you were ... um ...having...ah...?"

"That's right," she said. "And I'd love to with you." "Sounds great to me," I replied as evenly as I could, all the while thinking, This is too easy.

The problem was where to go. Fortunately, one of my fellow pilots was aware of our relationship, and when I told him what she had said, he suggested that I borrow his car and take this sexy WAC to a motel.

The next night we drove to a tavern for a few drinks. This would be my first time with a woman, I was very nervous, and I needed the alcohol to calm me down. She must have sensed that, because she took the initiative. We got into my friend's car, and she told me where to go.

"Turn up here," she told me.

I turned onto a very narrow street. As we drove down it, we heard bumping noises.

"Boy, they sure do need to fix this road," I muttered. "Maybe there's something under the car," my date suggested. I got out of the car and saw what looked like railroad ties under it. What are they doing there? I wondered. I looked ahead and saw that not only had I turned the car onto a railroad track, I had driven down it for about 50 yards.

Embarrassed and frustrated, I got back into the car and told my date what had happened. As I backed the car back to the road, the liquor was making its presence known in my stomach with every bump we made over the railroad ties. By the time the car was back on the street, I felt too sick to do anything. We drove back to Maxwell Field. I intended to make it up to her, but

I was transferred from Maxwell a few days later, and that was the end of that romance.

My life changed when I became a lieutenant and a pilot, and I felt that my transitional training helped me to get used to that adjustment. Needless to say, I enjoyed my second stay at Maxwell much more than I did my first, and as I packed to leave for Westover Field, I thought over these past three months.

There was Mr. Thurman, someone with whom I could associate home. There was Captain Gillis, my mentor as a B-24 pilot. There was the freedom associated with being an officer. And there was a pretty WAC who might have meant something more to me, but who was probably already falling in love with the next officer. I decided that I was leaving for Springfield, Massachusetts with mixed emotions.

## Combat Crew Training

Soon after I arrived at Westover Field in September 1944, I became the first pilot of a crew of ten airmen, and we trained together for combat bombing. All of the airmen who became members of my crew were no older than twenty-one and from the North. They were amused at having a rebel first pilot, but I reminded them that Southerners were natural leaders anyway, so it was appropriate.

Lieutenant Kenneth Elliott was a young man from Missouri who served as our copilot. He was an excellent pilot and a good crew member. Lieutenant Eugene Calhoun, our navigator, was a well qualified navigator from Illinois. A native of Connecticut, Peter C. George was our flight officer and bombardier. We soon learned that he could always bull's-eye the target, and that gave us a tremendous amount of confidence.

Sergeant Jack Keeley, our flight engineer, was from Massachusetts. It was his job to keep us constantly informed on how our engines were performing, and I always felt safe when he was aboard. Another valuable crew member was Sergeant John

Carnevale from Massachusetts. He was our radio operator and second navigator, and he always kept our radio equipment in perfect operation. Rounding out our crew was Sergeant George Philbrick from Maine.[3]

Philbrick was originally trained to be our waist gunner, but when we began flying covert combat missions, his role switched to that of dispatcher. He saw to it that men and supplies were successfully dropped from our plane to the underground, and his performance was perfect.

I was pleased to see that our non-commissioned crew members did their jobs exceptionally well, considering their youth. If they had been a little older I believed most of them could have been commissioned pilots. Nevertheless, we were all proud of the make-up of our crew, and we became close friends.

My crew members were serious in their training. We learned bombing, high-altitude (20,000 feet) and low-altitude (500-1,000 feet), the latter which we practiced over a small island off the Massachusetts coast. We also learned how to navigate the large aircraft, as well as how to fly it in formation. A final aspect of our training involved flying over the ocean near Long Island to give our gunners a chance to practice shooting their 50 caliber guns.

Approximately fifteen crews were in our group for training, but after several weeks of training it was clear that some of them didn't have enough discipline to keep up the training schedules.. We were all young men, but youth can't excuse everything, and our squadron commander felt that they were goofing off too much.[4] Entire crews would miss their flights because

---

3  Corporal George Wietzel, ball turret gunner from Detroit, and Corporal Leonard Kanehl, nose gunner, also trained with us at Westover Field. They were stationed with us in England, but since we flew covert support missions, they weren't needed on board.

4  A few men were simply in no hurry to go overseas. Our original tail gunner refused to go to England with us, despite the fact that he had done well in training and had just been promoted. When a major and I tried to talk some sense into him, he ripped his new stripes off

they "overslept", or some other excuse. Finally, he gave a lecture to express his "serious concern for the lack of progress" that most crews had made.

"Do you realize," he asked us, "that some of you are weeks behind completing all of your requirements? What are you going to do when you get overseas and you screw up in combat because you were too busy goofing off at Westover?"

The commander went on to say that higher command was disturbed over their progress, and he insisted that the crews do better. As an incentive, he revealed an offer made by the administrative officers. The first crew to complete all requirements would get a week of leave. Higher command thought that competition would result in greater performance for all crews. The bulletin board showed that our crew was in first place when the challenge was made.

Challenges were things I understood well. Throughout my youth my siblings and I learned how to be competitive. We had to be if we wanted to be accepted in the new places we were constantly moving to. The desire to be the best, coupled with the discipline I had learned, made me stay on top of my crew. I was going to make sure we got our leave. I didn't realize I was working them so hard until they told me that they were going to nickname our plane "The Whip".

I took that as a compliment. Unfortunately, my navigator didn't mean it that way.

One day our operations officer informed me that Eugene Calhoun did not report for instructions in operating the nose gun. These instructions were essential, because the navigator would have to operate the gun if the nose gunner was wounded or killed during a combat situation. It was my responsibility to notify Calhoun that he had to complete the gunnery instructions.

---

his sleeve, threw them in the major's face and roared, "you keep this damn promotion!" Sergeant Frank Stevenson was assigned to my crew as a result, and he became our tail gunner on our combat missions.

"Calhoun," I said when I found him, "the operations officer just told me that you didn't receive your instructions for shooting the nose gun. You need to get that taken care of."

Suddenly, he exploded in anger.

"Listen, Fes," he growled, "I have the same rank as you, and you can't give me orders to do a damn thing. I'm no gunner, and I'm not gonna do it!"

"This isn't my order, Calhoun, and you know it," I fired back. "The operations officer ordered me to tell you to report, so why not just calm down and do it? If you don't, you may get in trouble."

Calhoun abruptly stalked off, leaving me to wonder about the future of our relationship and how it might affect the crew. I knew that I would not tolerate insubordination aboard my plane, and I hoped his attitude would improve.

I never found out if he completed the gunnery requirement. There were many days of bad weather at Westover that kept us grounded, and it was during one of those days that Elliott and I assumed there would be no flights that night. We needed something to do, so we decided to join a poker game and drink. The game had just warmed up, and we had downed a few drinks when a messenger notified us that we would make a night navigational flight within the hour.

"Once we get airborne," I told Elliott, "we'll put the plane on auto pilot. But let's be sure to keep each other awake. Talk to me, I don't care about what."

Elliott agreed, and we soon took off.

We put the plane on auto pilot after we had flown for about an hour. Elliott and I tried to keep our pledge, but the drone of the engines and the relaxing effects of the alcohol were too much for us, and we were soon asleep.

Suddenly I felt someone shaking me roughly. It was Calhoun. "I tried to contact you by intercom," he growled, obviously angry. "Do you realize we're 30 miles off course? I had to crawl up here to tell you that!"

I pulled myself together. "All right, I'll take care of it."

Calhoun said nothing, but huffed off back to his position in the nose of the plane. Two embarrassed pilots made the necessary course correction. It was bad enough to be caught sleeping at the controls, but even worse to be caught by Calhoun. I wondered if he would report me, then decided that if he did, I could always ask if he had completed his gunnery requirement. Silently I vowed that this would be the only time I would sleep at the controls.

Other than those two situations, our training went without a hitch. There were a few attempts made by other crews to catch up to us, but for the most part the race to complete the training first was a joke. We had completed all phases of combat training a month ahead of everybody else, so there was no real contest. The timing was perfect: most of my crewmen could be home for Christmas, since almost all of them were from New England states. A few were thrilled about seeing hometown girl friends. Unfortunately, Tennessee was too far away for me to consider going home.

The day after we completed our combat training, I went to the group commander's office to arrange for our leaves, only to get a hell of a shock.

"I'm sorry, Lieutenant," the colonel said, "but the offer of leaves was canceled."

I stared at the colonel, unable to believe it.

"Your crew has been put on special orders by a general in Washington, D. C. Your assignment is secret, and will be disclosed to you later."

I found my voice.

"We appreciate the general's confidence, Colonel. But my crew is expecting a leave of some sort. Isn't there anything you can do?"

The colonel thought about it, then replied that we could take leave if everyone could return within a twenty-four hour notice.

"Don't take this the wrong way, Lieutenant Fesmire," he said. "Your crew has done extremely well, and I think you'll find these orders to be in your best interest."

I saw that a day's leave was the best I was going to get, and I returned to pass the news on to the crew.

To say that the crew was disappointed and hurt would be an understatement: in military terms they were pissed off. But after they calmed down, some of them were ready to take off for home. They were just about to leave when I received a notice for our crew to report within an hour to a photographic center on the base. It was lucky that all of us were available.

We were surprised. Each of us was given a civilian sport coat, shirt, and tie. After we had put them on, we had individual photos made. We received our photos that afternoon, and we were to keep them for a special use.

"Fesmire," one of them asked, "what the hell is going on?" "I wish I knew," I replied.

A couple of my crew looked at their packed bags, debating over whether or not to risk going off base.

"What if we get on a train and they call us back?"

"Don't know."

"Maybe you should wait until morning," I suggested. "I'll go to the Colonel's office first thing and find out for certain if you can go." Everyone else thought that was a good plan, so they settled down and decided to wait.

I went to the base commander the next day, and he still couldn't reveal any information about our assignment.

"But you can go home," he said. "However, you must be sure you can get back within a 24 hour notice. That's the best I can do."

I went back to the crew and told them what the colonel had said. "Give me your phone numbers, and I'll call you if something comes up," I said. Those that lived close did so and immediately left for home.

During late afternoon of the next day our crew received the order to ship out within twenty-four hours. I hurriedly made phone calls and told everyone to get back in a rush. Everyone got back to the base on time except for Sergeant Philbrick, who had to come back from visiting his girlfriend in Maine. It was a close call, but he reported within twenty-four hours. Our colonel found out that Philbrick missed an early briefing. Without an inquiry, he issued an order to demote an innocent man. He was only an hour late, but for some reason our head colonel found out about it and sent a request that he be court-martialed.

"But why?" I asked the major who had told me.

"Says that Philbrick left the base when he wasn't supposed to," the major replied.

"That's just not true, Major," I sputtered. "That colonel is stupid! Philbrick is one of the best men on my crew. He was doing exactly what he was allowed to do."

The major smiled. "I thought something wasn't right about this. How about I just file this paper in the trash? That way Philbrick's record will be clean."

I grinned. "Thank you, Sir."

As soon as that matter was cleared up, we left Westover Field for Mitchell Field, New York. We still had no idea what was in store for us.

Mitchell Field is an air base close to Hempstead, New York, and we arrived there in late December, 1944. All we were told for the next few days was that we were on a 24-hour alert. We didn't know what for, but we knew that it was not a typical situation. So for two weeks at Mitchell Field, all we had to do was eat, sleep, and sightsee, and this kid from the South was thrilled with the chance to visit New York City. I had not been out of Tennessee prior to entering active duty, and had never been in a city this size. So this time in the Big Apple was a special thrill.

One day during our two week stay at Mitchell Field, Calhoun ended up in the hospital. He didn't show up one morning, and I wondered where he was. An officer told me that Calhoun had been admitted to the hospital the previous day. I rushed over to find out what had happened.

Calhoun was in the middle of a bridge game when I caught up with him. He glanced up at me as I entered the room, then back down at his cards.

"Heard you were sick," I said to him. "What's wrong?"

He kept his eyes on his hand. "Flu," he replied shortly."

"I'm sorry about that," I said, trying to ignore the tension between us.

Suddenly he turned to me. "Why didn't you come sooner?" he demanded hotly.

I was taken aback by his outburst, but just for a moment.

"Because I just found out about it, that's why! You were admitted, but no one told me what had happened until this morning. I came as soon as I could."

Calhoun mumbled something and looked back at his cards. The other men at the table sat quietly, and uncomfortably. I sensed it was time to cut the visit short.

"Anyway, I just wanted to check on you and see if you were doing all right. You need anything?"

"No. I'll be out soon." He looked up at me. "But thanks."

Thanks? I tried not to show surprise over his improved attitude.

"Anytime," I replied. "Get well soon. We need a good navigator."

His mood improved by the time I left.

A few days after Calhoun was back from the hospital, all of us were standing around the bulletin board catching up on the news.

"Look!" one of my men cried, pointing excitedly to a notice on the board. "It's a party!"

I read it. An apparently wealthy family wanted to host a party for all of the men on a B-24 crew.

"Want me to call?" I asked the men. They responded with a cheer, and I set off to find a phone.

The party took place in a beautiful mansion, and it was some party. No parents or servants were around, there was plenty of liquor, live music was provided, and there was a spacious dance floor. But the best part was the number of beautiful, young girls.

We danced, drank, and smooched the night away. I had a beautiful and sexy partner who looked even more beautiful and sexy with every drink and dance. She must have thought the same of me, because she finally took me by the hand and guided me to the room where the wine and liquor were stored.

"What do you think?" she asked me when she had shut the door.

I looked around at the racks of bottles and the single bench off to one side.

"About the wine?" I asked

She giggled. "No, the bench."

I looked at the bench again, still not comprehending what she meant. She drew me to her by way of explanation.

"I mean," she said, "that we could have some fun on the bench."

I don't see how we can fit, I thought.

"Sounds like fun to me," I replied.

We sat down together on the bench and began to kiss and caress each other. Suddenly I heard a soft click and watched in horror as a shaft of light widened inside the room.

"Whoops! Sorry!"

Both the girl and I bolted to an upright position when we heard the door open, and by the time the person was inside we were standing up. I didn't see who broke up our private party, but I do know that whoever it was caused a passionate couple to cool off fast.

If I thought my luck had turned sour at that party, Leonard Kanehl's surely had turned worse. Somehow he had broken a glass and cut his arm severely enough to require 40 stitches. I was worried first for his safety, then that he might have to be replaced as our nose gunner.

But my concern evaporated the next morning when I visited Kanehl. The major who had stitched his arm up showed me his handiwork and assured me that Kanehl could be ready to leave with us at any time. He could receive follow-up treatment at the next base.

"You know," the major added as I turned to go, "I have no worries about your crew. You'll come through this war together just fine."

"Thank you for saying so, major," I replied, somewhat puzzled.

"What I mean," he went on as if he sensed my question, "is that you must be perfectly compatible for all ten of you to attend a party together."

I thought about that, and it made me feel good.

The next day we were given a short notice to pack our belongings and report to the operations office. The only information we received was that we would take off in a new B-24 for Bangor, Maine. I was curious about what we would wind up doing, but not overly so. We were too young to be impressed with the secrecy.

## Route to Secrecy

It was early January, 1945 when we received special orders to leave Mitchell Field for our combat assignment, and no briefing was given when we left. We flew a new B-24 to Bangor, Maine, where we received some indoctrination, physicals, and spent a busy two days. All of us were issued clothing for cold weather flying, a .45 Army pistol, and other equipment.

Although my father was a Methodist minister, religion hadn't entered my mind from the first day I had gone on active duty. I found that I had little time to go to church, and I also had become disillusioned with some of the chaplains on other bases. As an officer, I saw them in the same bars I went to. That may have been hypocritical, but I felt that a minister should set an example, and I couldn't respect a chaplain who could out drink me. But we had a very meaningful religious experience with a Baptist chaplain from Chattanooga, Tennessee.

The chaplain had what amounted to a brief service with our crew. He told us to keep the Lord on our minds, even when things looked bad for us. He then asked us to hold hands while he prayed.

Both the words and the man had a great effect on me. Listening to him was like listening to my dad: the two men seemed to share the same philosophy. After thanking him very much, I told him I was a Methodist minister's kid from Tennessee and that it sure was good to see someone else from home.

I wrote a quick letter to my parents to tell them about this experience. I reassured them that everything was okay and for them not to worry.

The next day we took off for Goose Bay, Labrador. Shortly after we were airborne I had a thought.

"Say, Philbrick," I called. "Don't you live in Maine?" "Fairfield," he replied. "Do you think we can fly over?" "Calhoun?" I called to our navigator.

"It's close enough," he replied.

We adjusted our course. When we were over the town I dropped our altitude to around 500 feet, circled around their home, and waved the plane's wings. Philbrick stared out of the windows in quiet excitement as we flew over his hometown.

"Thanks, Chief," he said as we turned back to our original course.

We arrived at Goose Bay in early January, 1945. Six feet of snow was on the ground and the temperature was -30°. It was an amazing sight to this 21-year-old from Tennessee. We spent the night, refueled, then took off for Iceland. The flight took us over the coast of Greenland, which proved to be another breathtaking experience. We had perfect weather, and the mountains glistening with ice and snow were beautiful from the air. We saw several B-24s and B-17s flying the same route.

After an overnight stay at Iceland, we flew to Prestwick, Scotland. The next day, we had a train ride to the Carpetbagger base at Harrington where we were finally briefed on the significance of our special orders.

We would be involved in the secret war against Hitler.

# 4

# The Secret War

During World War II, folks back home knew about what was going on overseas from the newspapers and newsreels—the raids, the bombing missions, and so on. And to be sure, most of the Eighth Air Force (the division to which I was assigned) was part of those activities. Three of our Carpetbagger squadrons, the 857th, 858th and 859th of the 801st/492nd Bomb Group, did some night bombing with black B-24s. Sometimes their bombs were only propaganda leaflets, but other times perhaps fifteen to twenty of our planes would fly as decoys for RAF bombers on joint missions. As the British planes neared their target, the decoy aircrafts would veer off course and drop aluminum chaff. The metal particles confused German radar, and the planes served to direct their anti-aircraft fire away from those carrying the real bombs. These squadrons were like "Jack of all Trades." They did everything.

The public didn't and couldn't know about the overwhelming amount of covert activity by underground forces in countries occupied by Germany. Their activity was very important in Hitler's defeat, but they had to have a constant and reliable source of weapons and supplies. That job was the primary responsibility of the 856th squadron in our 801st/492nd Bomb Groups.[5] Thousands of flights of B-24s dropped canisters over occupied countries. These canisters, floated down by parachutes, provided the materials the underground needed to continue the secret war. Many OSS agents were also dropped to become involved in the covert action.

Now I understood what the colonel at Westover Field had meant by this assignment being in our best interest. Our crew had finished first among approximately twenty crews in bomb training, and all of us were competitive. It gave us a great sense of satisfaction to know that we were delivering material and supplies that helped underground fighters undermine the Nazi effort, and we were pleased to be assigned to the 856th Squadron in the Carpetbagger Group at Harrington.

I was especially pleased to be a Carpetbagger. As a bomber pilot in formation combat flying, I would be like a robot. Moreover, I would have to rely on other, unfamiliar crews to do their jobs, and I always preferred doing it myself. I was a maverick, and as chief of a Carpetbagger plane on a lone mission, I could make my own major decisions.

During January, 1945, our crew received some daylight training in making low-altitude night drops of military supplies. The bomb bay on each black B-24 had been modified to hold containers instead of bombs. The containers were filled with an assortment of guns, ammunition, and other supplies for the

---

5  The Carpetbagger group included personnel from the 492nd and the 801st Bomb Groups. The official designation of this maverick group was established after several post-war years. Also, we did not know the code name "Carpetbaggers" until the end of the war.

underground. The ball turret was taken out of the B-24's waist, and the hole fitted with a removable cover. OSS agents parachuted to their targets through this hole, sometimes referred to as the Joe hole. No crew training in night drops of men contributed to some tragedies, however, each opperation of this type against the Germans was apparently successful.

Pete George, our bombardier, was positioned in the nose, where he had a better view of the target than I had. It was his responsibility to put us over the target and trigger the drop mechanism. If we had to make minor course corrections, he guided us by referring to the target's relative position on a clock face. His guidance and timing were critical. If we had to circle and hunt for the target, we risked exposure to the German guns.

George Philbrick, our dispatcher, always checked the bomb bay before every flight to make sure it would operate properly when it was time for the drop. He also had the responsibility of timing the drops of agents through the Joe hole in the waist. The cord that opened each man's parachute was tied to a line within the plane. As the agent dropped through, the line would automatically open the chutes. Philbrick not only had to make sure the men got through as fast as possible, he had to coordinate the jumps so that neither lines nor chutes got tangled. Both men worked well as a team and always made perfect drops.

All missions were flown at night, and drops were made from a few hundred feet above the ground. The underground resistance fighters turned on the signal lights as soon as they heard the roar of our plane and saw the outline of our black B-24 when it approached the target.

Earlier Carpetbagger crews had to learn on their own how to be successful in flying the secret night missions of dropping agents and supplies to the underground, and to a large extent so did we. The veteran crews were able to give us some limited training, though not much. We practiced low-altitude flying during daylight hours, not under actual conditions.

The squadron bombardier also worked with flight officer George on timing his drops, and we got the chance to make a single practice cargo drop over the airfield.[6] We quickly learned the difference between dropping ordinance that fell straight down and dropping cargo containers with parachutes, and if I had been older I would have thought more about the danger involved to both the agents we dropped and to us. But we were young and didn't appreciate the fact that we had received little training.

I believe that the best training for my being successful as a Carpetbagger came during my teenage years when I had to rely on myself to earn my room, board, and education. I was a maverick who didn't hesitate to make a critical decision. On a few occasions when I thought the order of a commanding officer was wrong, I ignored the order. Fortunately, everything always worked out for the best.

What we lacked in training was made up for by our intelligence officer prior to each mission. OSS headquarters in London had super radio communications with the underground in the Nazi-occupied countries. They relayed German gun positions to our intelligence officer and he marked them on a map. The flight plan was never a straight line from our base to the target. Since we had no means of defending ourselves against heavy enemy fire, we flew around the guns, sometimes going miles out of our way to do so. The cover of night and our low altitude also helped conceal us from anti-aircraft fire. Lieutenant Calhoun was a terrific navigator who skillfully guided us out of range. But this is not to say that we never saw any flack. We were exposed to our share of enemy fire, but we survived.

Our commanders lectured us not to discuss our missions with anyone. Nor could we receive guidance while in the air. On each

---

6   Sergeant Philbrick made agent drops on a signal by the bombadier.

mission we would be strictly on our own, and I had the ultimate responsibility of deciding the success or failure of each mission. I was glad that my early years had prepared me to think fast on my feet.

One day after such a lecture on secrecy, I walked to a small latrine approximately 200 feet from our hut. I was about to open the door when someone called out from inside.

"Wait, Yank, I'll be through in a minute!"

What startled me and briefly made me forget my discomfort was the fact that the voice belonged to a British female.

I was used to English locals on the base. Most of them were men doing carpentry work, painting, pouring concrete, or other maintenance tasks. A few women were here also, probably as secretaries. But this area was strictly off-limits to non-military personnel, and I had no idea how she could have managed to be here.

But secrecy and security didn't matter to me much then. I just had to go.

"Hurry it up!"

Later I learned that a few men in our Carpetbagger group could always figure out some way to get women into the hut for sex. Another pilot told me that the girl was a civilian worker with a security clearance for our base. She frequently spent the night with some of our officers.

Ever since I joined the military I had had the chance for sex with beautiful girls, but for some reason I wasn't able to follow through with my opportunities. You may be unlucky with women, I thought, but at least you've never gotten venereal disease.

The veteran pilots were able to pass on to us their advice and tactics. Several of them had flown missions every night, weather permitting. They described the tracer effect of enemy fire, or how the paths of the bullets would light up the sky at night. Their stories sobered our thoughts about the mission, and if we were ever motivated to stay on course to avoid the German guns, we were even more so now.

On the morning of February 28, 1945, our crew was notified that we would fly our first night mission over Nazi-occupied Denmark. That afternoon we were briefed on the responsibilities of each crew member. Our target lay about 50 miles inside Denmark from the North Sea coast.

Lieutenant Calhoun plotted a flight plan to avoid enemy gun positions. Flying at 500 feet during the night and being on course over Denmark, we hoped to have no problem from German ground fire. We were told that German night fighter planes were of less danger to us at a low altitude.

After we had flown for about ten minutes over enemy territory, we saw some tracer fire. It looked like 50 caliber, but it was of minimum danger to us. The intelligence briefing was accurate, and Calhoun did a perfect job of keeping us on course. Eventually we saw the target lights turned on by the Danish patriots. We made our drop, did a quick 180 degree turn, and headed back to base.

As we crossed the Channel, it suddenly struck us that we had remained perfectly calm throughout the mission. Each of us had a job to think about, and the tracer fire looked more like a Fourth of July show. We were pleased that we weren't worried, and by the time the flight was over we felt like a veteran crew.

We arrived back at our Carpetbagger base at daylight. The officers reported for an intelligence debriefing, during which we were served fine Scotch liquor. We drank a toast, made our report, then headed to the mess hall for breakfast.

My adrenaline had me so pumped up that I didn't bother catching up on any sleep during the daytime. I had been awake over 24 hours. But by 8:00 that evening, I could stand it no longer, and I went to bed early. I was asleep within minutes.

Then, from out of nowhere I heard several loud explosions. Tracer fire, I thought. Close. Awfully close.

Suddenly I sat bolt upright in bed. I shook my head to clear it of the remains of so vivid a dream. I slowly realized that I had been dreaming about the mission, and it scared the hell out of me. I looked around, grateful to be in my hut. But those explosions had sounded so real.

I soon found out why. We had a copilot from Texas in our hut who was wild, and we had learned to expect anything from him. That evening, for no apparent reason, he fired three rounds from his .45 through the ceiling. He was drunk, and we took the pistol away from him. I had trouble sleeping the rest of the night.

All of us had been issued Army .45 pistols before leaving the states, but we weren't surprised the next morning when a GI came into our hut and handed us a copy of an order from Colonel Rodman St. Clair, our squadron commander. The order directed us to turn all pistols into his office by 3:00 that afternoon. It was a good idea, since we didn't take them on missions anyway.

Most of our combat crews were made up of young men in their early twenties, and some pulled some crazy stunts when they were on base. But during missions they were deadly serious and took pride in the fact that they were making the secret war against Hitler a success.

The weather during the next few days proved unsuitable for combat action, but our intelligence officer told me that our first mission was a success. The communication with the underground was amazing. Our Carpetbagger group had dropped an abundant supply of military equipment to the patriots in Nazi occupied countries.

By March 5, the weather finally cleared up enough for our second night mission over Denmark. We would be over Nazi occupied territory for about an hour while we dropped more military supplies to the underground.

As before, we saw the German artillery fire from the ground. Our intelligence report had accurately predicted their location;

our flying around them was safer. But this time there was a clear sky and a full moon, and the two combined to give a dusk like appearance to the ground below. We looked up and saw two German night fighters flying above and around us.

"Look up there, Elliott," I said to my copilot. He looked to where I was pointing.

"Damn! Think they've seen us?"

"Hope not," I replied as I pushed the plane's controls forward. I dropped our altitude to 200 feet. Our airspeed was 180 miles per hour, and I knew that the fighters could outrun us easily.

"There, now," I said. "I doubt they'll risk flying so low." But we still kept an eye on them.

After a few tense minutes, we were free of them. We made a routine drop, returned to base, and gave our debriefing, once again over Scotch. After breakfast, I felt the effects of lack of sleep, and unlike before, I went straight to bed and slept soundly.

After only a few hours of sleep I was awakened at 11 a.m. by a messenger.

"What is it?" I mumbled sleepily.

"Sorry, Sir," he replied. "You have another mission tonight. Colonel wants a briefing."

"Okay," I yawned. I got up, stretched, and thought, What a refreshing three hours!

During our briefing I learned we were to drop the usual military supplies over Denmark. The mission itself was uneventful for the most part. There were no fighters, no enemy fire, and no deviation from course.

Finally we arrived at the target area.

"Anybody see the lights?" I asked. No one did.

"Calhoun, this is the target area, right?"

"According to the map," Calhoun replied. "Maybe they can't turn them on yet."

We circled around the area several times, but could see no signs of the lights.

Suddenly Pete George called out, "Lights ahead, one o'clock!"

We all looked out and made sure they were the target lights. Satisfied, we made our drop, then flew back to base.

During our usual morning toasts, we reported the problem with the lights to our intelligence officer. He thanked us, then dismissed us for breakfast and rest. We slept most of the morning.

We weren't scheduled for a mission that night, so I spent some time at the officer's bar. When I got back, an English girl and one of our pilots bolted from my bunk and hastily pulled their clothes back on. From the looks on their faces I'm sure they had just enough time to finish before I discovered them.

"Something wrong with your bed?" I snapped. The pilot and the girl had the grace to be embarrassed, and they left without reply. Disgusted, I hastily changed the blanket on the bed. I observed that either very few of our men were involved in this kind of activity, or they were more discrete than this fellow.

After an extra day of rest we received a late afternoon notice on 8 March to fly an important mission to Copenhagen, Denmark. Unfortunately, copilot Ken Elliott and I had spent some time that day in the officer's club bar. We had assumed no flight that night, and had downed a couple of drinks. By the time we were ready for takeoff, both he and I felt the effects of the alcohol, but we told no one.

Copenhagen is on the eastern edge of Denmark, and it would be our longest mission to date. I felt drowsy from the Scotch, and I was sure Elliott did. I pulled him aside before we boarded the plane.

"You keep me talking," I said, "and I'll do the same for you. That way we'll stay awake." He agreed.

This time we were able to keep ourselves from dozing off, and we flew without incident until we were several miles from the drop area.

"Hey! Look at that!" George called out.

Ahead of us the whole sky over Copenhagen was lit up by anti-aircraft fire, and it looked like the city was under an umbrella of spectacular colors. It could have been a fireworks celebration, except that the reports were too loud.

We headed directly for our drop area, and what I thought was beautiful only moments ago was threatening now, and quickly becoming worse. Fortunately, we were able to fly directly over our target and make a successful drop. Elliott and I were thoroughly awake and sober by this time, and we turned and headed back for base.

During the debriefing we reported the excitement we had seen over Copenhagen. Our intelligence officer was ready with an explanation.

"Shortly after you took off," he began, "OSS in London contacted our intelligence group with an order to cancel your flight. Royal Air Force bombers had planned a very important, low bombing operation for tomorrow night. But the weather forecasts predicted clouds, and they had to fly their mission last night, same time you were there. I tried to radio you, but you must have been out of range."

About ten days after our Copenhagen mission, I learned the purpose of the RAF bombing. An important Danish underground leader spoke to us about the covert activities taking place in his homeland. He revealed the success of the RAF low-altitude bombing of a prison compound in Copenhagen which allowed many Danish patriots to escape. He expressed great appreciation for our group's support in their secret war against Hitler.

After the Copenhagen mission, we were hoping to have a few free nights, but it didn't happen. We flew another successful mission over Denmark during the night of March 9. It was a good drop, and there was no enemy fire. But even though it was routine, it had more meaning to me than any other mission I flew.

I was exhausted from lack of sleep, and during most of the mission we had cloud cover above us that blocked the moonlight, and gave the features on the ground a dull appearance. Suddenly we entered an area of perfectly clear sky with a beautiful moon shining brightly. I was flying at about 500 feet and could see several features of the ground distinctly.

We were over a small village when I looked down at the terrain. I saw a white painted church with a tall steeple. It looked exactly like the beautiful Methodist church in Nolensville, Tennessee where my father was pastor. I suddenly felt a strange feeling inside me, and to this day I can only describe it as a spontaneous religious experience. This was the first time I had even thought about religion in several months.

I thought about the church all the way back to our base, throughout the debriefing, breakfast, and as I was getting ready to sleep. Later that morning a messenger woke me.

"Lieutenant, the chaplain wants to see you."

My eyes were open in an instant, and the memory of the church came flooding back.

"I'll be right there," I said as I swung out over the edge of the bed. I felt as though I had received a message from above.

When I got to the chaplain's office, he invited me to sit down.

"I received a letter from your parents," he began.

"Are they all right?" I asked.

"They're fine, Lieutenant, but they tell me that they haven't received word from you in several weeks, and that they're worried about you. If you could spare a few minutes, I'm sure they'd love to hear from you."

"Yes, Sir. I'll write them as soon as I can." "Immediately, would be better, Lieutenant. I'm sure that every day for them that goes by without a letter makes them feel worse."

"Yes, Sir."

I left his office feeling guilty, but believing that these events were so perfectly synchronized that they must have been sent by God. I was motivated to do better.

I wrote my father about the church I had seen, and how much it reminded me of his back home. I added for them not to worry. I was fine, but all of our letters were censored, and there wasn't much I could say about what was going on over here. I sealed the letter and mailed it, knowing that they were the greatest parents anyone could have, and that they would understand.

I had just finished writing when I got a message that the intelligence officer wanted to see our flight officers.

"I just wanted to let you guys know that your last mission was successful," he told us when we had assembled in his office. "And I have some bad news to pass on. The mission you flew three nights ago was a disaster for the underground."

"Did we miss the target?" I asked.

"No, the drop was just fine. But because you had to circle for so long, the Germans were alerted to your presence. What happened wasn't your fault. The Danish waited until morning to retrieve the supplies, but the Germans had gotten there first. They planted explosives in the canisters, and some of the underground were killed."

There was nothing we could say. We deeply regretted the loss of life, but under the circumstances there was nothing else we could have done. I had been ready to abort the mission when the lights had come on. I shook my head.

"Here's something that will make you feel better," the intelligence officer went on. "I've just learned that your crew is the most successful one in the group. Congratulations."

We left his office, and I vowed to make sure that another incident like the one that resulted in the deaths of the Danish freedom fighters never happened again.

We had been flying missions almost every night, and we were exhausted. But fortunately we had a full week to recover after our fifth mission. We used the time to catch up on our sleep, eat, and play bridge.

By March 16 we were ready for our sixth covert mission. It was uneventful, except for some tracer fire by the Germans.

Lieutenant Calhoun kept us more than a mile away from the guns, and they posed no danger to us. The trip back to the base was just as routine, and we really felt like seasoned veterans now.

"Sir," I said to our intelligence officer during our debriefing, "I just want to say that we owe our success to the intelligence you provide. The gun positions are always accurately marked on the maps we have."

He shook his head.

"I could give the best intelligence in the world to crews," he replied, "and a few of them could still screw up a mission. No, you make your success, and we're grateful. In fact, since you've flown six missions, you'll be awarded air medals."

The medal ceremony was a formal event, and we were proud in having earned them. Colonel St. Clair was in charge of the ceremony.

We had four days of rest because of unsuitable weather conditions. During my liberty, I took it easy as much as I could, probably drank too much, and got a haircut by an GI amateur barber. I also indulged myself in the luxury of daily showers.

I was shocked at what happened during one of these showers. It was a cool morning, and the hot water sure felt good. The building was large enough for several partitioned shower areas; even so, I thought that I was alone in the building.

Suddenly I heard the distinctive giggle of a female. I knew that this shower building was for males only, and I was reminded of the girl in our latrine I had almost walked in on. The giggling continued, and curiosity got the best of me. Completely naked, I walked around the partition to take a look.

One of the pilots was trying to have sex with an English girl. Both of them were naked and joined together in a way I had never imagined.

The pilot looked up, recognized me, and grinned.

"Want to share?" he offered politely.

I recovered my wits.

"No, thanks," I laughed. "Just having seen the show is enough for me." I dried off, dressed, and left. For a 21-year old virgin, I sure was learning a lot.

As I walked back to our hut, I began to wonder about the quality of our base's security. After all, we flew secret missions all the time, but several English citizens worked on the base daily. They took tea breaks during mid-morning and mid after-noon. A few of our young airmen must have convinced some of them that taking sex breaks was more fun. Nevertheless I was sure that these English civilians were checked carefully by secu-rity. There was little they could learn from the contents in our huts, and even if a pilot had talked, he could only have said where he had been, and the Germans probably knew that much. We never knew our destination until our briefing before takeoff. I was confident that these girls were not spies, and that nothing from our base would reach the Germans.

Our days of rest came to an end, and we flew another mission over the center of Denmark during the night of 20 March. We had become a veteran crew, and it amazes me now that we didn't dread flying combat missions then. But each of us had confidence that the rest of the crew would carry out their re-sponsibilities.

It was this teamwork that made our seventh mission over Denmark routine. We only saw one flash of tracer fire, and it was miles away. Debriefing was simple, and I reminded myself that we had completed all of our missions without a single abor-tion.

I was convinced that the hundreds of night missions our com-bat crews had flown over Denmark and Norway during this month alone could supply a whole army with military supplies. There were several other crews making similar flights, and I knew their payload capacity. They made flights every night the weather and moon permitted. So even if a small percentage of them had aborted, several thousand canisters of equipment reached the underground over the course of 2 months, and each one set the German war effort back even further.

We had three days of rest before our next mission. The food in the officer's mess was of the highest quality, and very delicious. While going through the serving line one evening, I saw large, juicy steaks. My mouth began to water as the private served it up on my plate. It was as good as it looked, too.

After I finished eating, I walked over to the mess sergeant. "Tell me something, sergeant," I asked him.

"Yes, Sir?"

"Where did you get such beautiful steaks?"

He smiled.

"Glad you like 'em. One of the planes here flies up to Ireland a lot. Ireland's neutral, see. Anyway, they buy beef, Scotch, and gin over there."

That explains the abundance of Scotch we have at every debriefing, I thought. I wonder if the guys in the rest of the Eighth Air Force eat and drink as well as we do.

"Well, it's the best food I've ever had. Keep it up."

"Yes, Sir."

While we enjoyed the best wartime food one could possibly eat, I couldn't help but feel guilty. The whole British population sacrificed greatly during World War II, and they suffered from malnutrition to the point that most local girls I saw had decayed teeth and unhealthy complexions. Nor were cosmetics available for the ladies to hide the symptoms of an unhealthy diet. But if they had not craved sweets as much as they did, I'm sure that their teeth would have been a little healthier.

We had 3 days of taking it easy. Then, on 23 March, we flew another uneventful mission over Denmark. Like before, the mission was followed by a debriefing, during which our intelligence officer praised us for having completed all of our drops without aborting. But unlike before, he didn't break out the Scotch. Instead, he suggested an immediate breakfast followed by sleep. He hinted that we might have a noon meeting, and would say nothing further.

# 5

# William Colby and the Norway Mission

It seemed that I had only been asleep for a short time when a messenger awoke me.

"Wake up, Sir. You have a briefing at 10:00."

I opened my eyes and looked at my watch. Only 2 hours of sleep out of the past 26. Why did we have to brief now if we had to wait until night to fly? We had become adjusted to flying two night missions in a row; however, we had been able to sleep until mid-afternoon before receiving a message to fly that night. I felt hung over from the loss of sleep.

The early briefing wasn't the only thing unusual. Eugene Calhoun, the navigator, and Pete George; our bombardier, were not ordered to attend; only Elliott and I were summoned. Whatever happened, I had the feeling that Calhoun would resent missing out on the action. The fact that so many high ranking officers were gathered together indicated the importance of the operation, and I quickly became alert.

When we entered the large briefing room, we saw almost one hundred people sitting around. Each crew sat together. We were joined by Captain Charles McGuire, navigator in the 856th Squadron, and Captain Robert France, 856th Squadron bombardier. I knew their records were excellent, and that they were the best at what they did.

About 30 men I had never seen before were grouped into a corner. They, along with military supplies, were to be dropped over northern Norway from our B-24s that night. As I watched the Joes, I could tell they would be successful in any type of military action. Every man had a quiet demeanor about him, but you could see the intelligence and determination in their eyes. They were all athletic and looked ready for the mission.

Major William Colby was their leader, and I soon learned that he and some of the men were to fly with our crew. We would be the lead crew, and I was pleased to be their pilot. I considered it an acknowledgment of my flawless record. I had also received recognition as a successful pilot by Captains McGuire and France.[7]

[None of the crews were briefed prior to takeoff on the significance of an operation. Only later did I learn the importance of the operation which Colby and his OSS men undertook. Their task was to blow up the railroad and bridges that went from northern Norway to the main portion of the country. A few hundred thousand troops that had escaped from the Russian front had taken this route into Norway, and Hitler wanted those forces back in Germany to boost the strength of his armies fighting the Allies. The successful destruction of railroad and bridges prevented German armies from getting back.]

---

7  I later found out that most of our crew were selected because we had successfully completed the missions we had flown.

I figured that after this mission was completed I would have two hours sleep out of fifty. Nevertheless, the adrenaline pumped through me, and I was excited.

The distance from our base to the drop site created the main difficulty of the mission. A B-24 could fly for only 10-11 hours, and it was at least a 14 hour flight between our base and the target. In the early afternoon of March 24, our planes left for a Royal Air Force airfield in Inverness, a town on the northern coast of Scotland. We would refuel there, then take off for the long journey to Norway. But even with the reduced distance, we still had to fly a 10 hour round trip to the Norwegian target and back. Between the extra weight and the unusually long flight, we knew that we barely had enough fuel to get to the target, make the drop, and return.

As we flew to the RAF air base, Captain France briefed Sergeant Philbrick on the procedure for dropping the men, and it was his responsibility to make sure they made successful jumps. Major Colby and I became better acquainted during the two hour flight to Inverness. I admired his professionalism, and he impressed me as a great leader. We discussed some of the details of our night flight.

When we landed at Inverness, I taxied to the ramp where a ground crewman directed me to park the plane in a grassy area. I was surprised at his directions, but could do nothing to object. Once the plane is on the ground, the ground crewman is in command. The pilot has to assume that ground control knows more about the overall conditions at the airfield. I parked, and we got out while the planes were checked and refueled.

After a short rest, my crew and the OSS men got back into the plane and readied ourselves for the long flight to Norway. Everything checked out, and I started the four engines. As I revved them up, the left wheel started to move, but not the right. I tried to move the plane again, but with the same luck. The weight of the men, supplies, and fuel was too much for the soft earth to support. I felt sick. Everyone's ready to go, I thought, and I'm stuck in the mud!

I called the control tower and informed them of the problem. I stopped the engines and all of us got out of the plane. The right wheel was buried deeper in the ground than I had feared, and it looked hopeless.

Our group colonel, along with several airmen and ground crews, gathered around the mired B-24. The colonel glanced at the aircraft, took in the situation, then looked directly at me.

"Lieutenant, don't you know better than to park a B-24 in the damn mud? What were you thinking?"

I was thinking that the ground crewman didn't know what the hell he was doing, as he went on bawling me out. I got boiling mad at him, but I didn't let on. I knew it wasn't my fault, and the colonel knew it wasn't my fault. But I could tell that he was afraid the mission would have to be aborted, and that he needed a scapegoat.

After he finished yelling at me, he turned to Major Colby. "Major," he said, "you get your men into the other planes. We'll just have to be a plane short."

"Colonel," he replied coolly yet firmly, "understand that I-not you—am in command of this operation. And I will abort it unless you get men to work and get this plane out of the mud."

The colonel looked ready to tear into Colby for insubordination, but he seemed to recognize that the major meant what he said, and I was tickled that the colonel kept his mouth shut. He turned to the ground crews.

"Well?" he snapped. "Stop standing around and get this plane out of the mud!"

The English ground personnel scrambled for shovels, and soon my plane was surrounded by men frantically digging me out. They quickly dug a sloping path for the right landing wheel. It was agreed that I would get on the plane alone for the attempt to free it.

I climbed in and started the engines. When they caught, I revved up the right ones much higher than the left ones. Thanks to the lighter load, the sloped trench, and the increased power, the right wheel jumped out of the hole. I didn't slow down until the plane was onto the pavement.

Once I was on pavement, I killed the engines, and everyone climbed aboard. We were almost an hour late because of the trapped wheel, but they gave us the green light anyway. I got into position for takeoff.

My anger toward the colonel was gone. I understood his dilemma: he was a highly respected man with a great combat record, and he always strived for success. But this time he was wrong. I knew it, and I thought he knew it, too.[8]

The Inverness control tower gave us clearance. Darkness was approaching, but it didn't bother me. I had learned to enjoy night flying. The runway lights had not yet been turned on, but I still could see the whole length of the runway. I opened up the throttles and roared down the runway.

Suddenly the lights came on along a cross runway, making the one I was on look like the wrong one. I had gotten used to the darkness, and the sudden bright lights in front of me blinded me. I didn't know what to do—was I even on the runway? Confused and scared, I pulled back on the controls and risked stalling out by getting airborne so quickly. We wobbled, but stabilized as our speed increased.

Just as I let out a sigh of relief, the tower called. "Sorry about that, mates," the British control officer on the other end said. "We turned on the wrong lights. Hope we didn't confuse you."

---

8 Several days after my flight to Norway, I learned that the colonel attempted a follow-up mission to drop men and supplies to Colby's group. He aborted the mission before he reached the frozen lake, reporting the weather was too bad to continue the flight.

The smooth British accent only angered me even more. "Hell yes, you confused us!" I shouted back. "We're damn lucky we didn't crash!"

"Whose side are they on, anyway?" Elliott muttered.

I snorted. This maverick was ready to be on his own while flying. I didn't want anybody telling me what to do or how to do it. But by the time we got across the North Sea, we were on our own, and I began to relax.

The five hour flight to the frozen lake in Norway was uneventful. During the time over the North Sea, Major Colby and I discussed how to make the drop.

"Listen, Fesmire," he said. "I need a low altitude drop, two, three hundred feet. Think you can do it?"

I didn't want to say no, but I wasn't an idiot, either. "Major, I'm concerned about those mountains we'll be flying toward. How about a thousand feet above the lake?"

Colby shook his head. "Too high. I want to make sure my men and supplies are on target. If we get scattered, we'll have to take the time to regroup, and I'd rather not do that."

Once again I thought of the mountain range we'd have to clear after we made the drop.

"I can drop you at five hundred feet if I think the conditions are right."

Colby grinned. "Deal," he said. He seemed to have confidence in me.

I admired Major Colby and his OSS team, and I was determined to drop him at five hundred feet. But if Colby had known what I knew about our crew's training and experience, he probably would have left us stranded back at Inverness. We had completed only three months of high-altitude bombing training before becoming Carpetbaggers. Our night flight training was limited, and we had received no training in dropping men. To further complicate our inexperience, some of us had had slept for only two hours out of the past forty. We had never flown a mission over Norway; and we didn't fully understand the dangers of the mountains. We just knew that they would be ahead of us and not to hit them.

Despite all of this, I tried my best to give Colby the impression that I knew what to do, that I was a pro. On the first count I think he gave me the benefit of the doubt. On the second, I'm sure he knew I wasn't.

Colby and I fell silent, and I began to think of how far I had come in two years. I had grown up in small towns, and had never been out of Tennessee until I was in active duty. In fact, I had spent less than twenty hours in driving an automobile. By now I had logged more than 1,000 hours as a pilot, most of them in a B24, and here I was—the lead pilot for an OSS mission in Norway. It had become a different world for me.

Talking with Colby and reminiscing made the long flight seem shorter. As we approached the drop zone, I was amazed at how well we could see the snow-capped mountains. It was a beautiful sight under a shining moon. Captain McGuire had us on a perfect course, and soon saw the large signal bonfire. I turned and headed for it.

When we were a few miles away, I lowered the flaps, changed the pitch of the propellers, and reduced the airspeed. I quickly lowered our altitude as much as I dared. Philbrick opened the Joe hole for the drop of the OSS men. He told them to wait for his signal so that their jumps would come at proper intervals.

We were about 500 feet over the frozen lake when we made our drops. Philbrick did a perfect job of coordinating the jumps, and Captain France dropped the supplies without incident. The whole thing was over within seconds, and we were delighted.

But there was no time to celebrate. A high, snow-covered peak was directly in front of us, and we were closing fast. How I did what I did next, I'll never know. I banked hard, flipping the plane almost upside down into a vertical and parallel path with the mountain, and turned 180 degrees in seconds. When it was over I looked at Elliott.

"How close did we come?" I asked him.

Elliott was silent for a long moment before he whispered, "At least a hundred feet."

I thought how lucky we were to be rid of the excess weight from the supplies and men; otherwise, we would not have made it. "Somebody was watching us tonight, men," I said. Silently, I thanked Captain Gillis at Maxwell for teaching me that maneuver.[9]

After we escaped the peak, I climbed to a safer altitude, and we began to feel better. Since there were no enemy planes or gunfire, we could take the time to take a closer look at Norway's terrain. The shining moon on the snow-covered mountain peaks was a beautiful sight.

The only concern that faced us now was the possibility of running out of gas. But Sergeant Keeley was a superb flight engineer, and he made sure that all of the engines were supplied with gas. He gave us regular reports on our fuel consumption and how much was left. By the time we touched down at Inverness we had about fifteen minutes of fuel remaining in the tanks.

We were the first plane to return to the Scotland airfield, and I was tired after forty-eight hours with two hours of sleep. We reported to intelligence and ate breakfast while our plane was serviced and refueled. After the two hour flight to our home base at Harrington, I was ready for bed. As I drifted off to sleep, I prayed for Colby's success against the German army in Norway.

Other crews made follow-up flights for this important operation throughout the next two weeks. We were ill-trained for

---

9 Approximately two weeks after we dropped Colby and his men, pilot Hudson crashed his B-24 into the same mountain peak we had missed, killing everyone on board. They were on a follow-up mission to drop additioanal OSS men and supplies for Colby's operation. We were saddened by the news. Hudson and the officers of his crew had lived in the same hut with our crew officers for three months. By a lucky accident, his original copilot had to sit out the fatal mission because of a fractured arm.

these missions, and these support flights were also hampered by the great distance to the target, bad weather, and mountainous terrain. They were not as successful as we had been, and I'll have to admit that a large portion of our success was due to luck.[10]

Whenever I got the chance, I enjoyed listening to Axis Sally over a radio in our hut. Her propaganda was hilarious. If hers was the only source of news, one would think that Germany was winning the war. But I learned about a screw-up involving Colby's Norwegian operation through Axis Sally's broadcasts. She revealed that Germany knew about a crew's mistake of dropping OSS men over neutral Sweden on 24 March. This much was true. Lieutenant Hudson's crew had missed the target and dropped thirty miles to the east. But it was obvious that Axis Sally didn't know the significance of this event to the operation in Norway. I knew Major Colby had been dropped on target, and I was sure of his success.

After our mission to Norway, I assumed that we would have a few days of rest. We arrived back at our home base around noon on 25 March, and I had the worst case of combat fatigue. I slept about twelve hours between late afternoon and early morning the next day, and that was almost all of the sleep I had since three days ago. And like before, I was awakened by messenger. I had to fly again that night.

I had recovered somewhat after half a day of sleep. Lieutenant Calhoun and Flight Officer George, my regular bombardier, rejoined us for this next mission. I was pleased to see our regular crew back together, although I was apprehensive about Calhoun. To give him due credit, there was no better navigator in

---

10 During another follow-up flight, Polinsky's crew, OSS personnel, and cargo perished when their plane crashed on the shore of northern Scotland. Like Lieutenant Hudson, Polinsky was flying with a substitute copilot. By a stroke of luck, regular copilot, Lieutenant John Lancaster was not on board, and he was later permanently assigned to my crew.

the Carpetbaggers, but he was a very aggressive person. He was the best at everything he did, and he made sure people knew about it, especially his superior officers. He felt like he was the captain of my plane, and he let me know it, too. I was sure that he was jealous because I had been singled out for the Norway mission, and his attitude showed it. But the fact of the matter was that OSS felt better having its most experienced navigator and bombardier on board Colby's plane.

Pete George, on the other hand, didn't care.

Our tenth combat mission on 26 March was uneventful, a welcome change from near misses with mountains and anti-aircraft fire. After we returned home, I slept until midday. When I awoke, I received a message to report to Colonel St. Clair, our squadron commander.

I walked into St. Clair's office and saluted him. He returned it, then said, "Fesmire, you have a great record in flying your combat missions. We are proud of you, and I'm pleased to inform you of your promotion to first lieutenant."

I tried to contain my excitement but failed.

"Thank you, Sir," I said through a grin.

St. Clair nodded, then resumed. "I have a great opportunity for you and your crew. I want you to listen carefully because I want you to volunteer for this assignment. I think you'll be pleased with it after I explain everything.

"Allied Command is proud of our clandestine operations, so much so that they want to establish the same sort of operation in China. I want you to fly your crew to the China theater. Your crew will train them in our methods of operation."

I was speechless. Colonel St. Clair must have interpreted it as uncertainty.

"I know you'll be pleased to volunteer," he went on. "It will be a great opportunity and an exciting experience. You should be eager to accept this opportunity."

I had found my voice by this time.

"Colonel, I appreciate the promotion very much," I said. "But let me understand you. Are you leaving it up to me to volunteer, or is this an order?"

"It's not an order, Fesmire," St. Clair replied. "But I'd like you to volunteer."

So it was an order to volunteer. I quickly evaluated my crew, and had to admit that a problem of attitude was present. I had known men who had been screwed when they had been eager to volunteer, and I felt we were more urgently needed in the European theater. Besides, I was happy here.

"Colonel," I said at last, "I have doubts about this. We are proud and happy to be under your command. We think we are doing a good job. If you want us to go to China, you'll have to give us a direct order. I will not volunteer."

The colonel's face turned red.

"Well, talk it over with your crew. I believe you and they will be willing to go."

But I knew the state of my crew's attitudes, and I quickly replied, "Sir, I'm sorry, but I prefer not to discuss the matter with my crew. I speak for them when I say I must decline your offer. If you want us to go, however, give the word."

St. Clair looked at me for a long minute before he said, "It's okay if you feel that way, Lieutenant. Dismissed."

I thanked Colonel St. Clair once again for the promotion before I left. As I walked back to my hut, I hoped that he wouldn't hold a grudge against me. He was a great person, and I respected him very much, but I knew that he really didn't want to accept the responsibility for ordering us to go. The base commander told him to pick a good crew, I reasoned, and with this recent Norway mission, we must have been first on the list. Besides, I had enough experience answering for goof-ups by higher ranking officers, and if Colonel St. Clair didn't want the responsibility, I wanted it even less.

I learned a few days later that another crew had gone to China in our place.

The day after my conference with Colonel St. Clair, we flew another mission over Denmark. I told no one of my upcoming promotion, and I assumed that no one was aware of the offer to go to China.

Our eleventh mission was routine. As usual, Calhoun guided us to the target area, and we made a successful drop. During the debriefing afterwards, it was obvious that the morale of our crew members had improved. I wondered if anybody had been notified of a promotion. Anyway, I was glad that everyone was happy.

# 6

# Separate Ways

The mission of March 28 was so routine that the crew actually seemed to enjoy the flight. Everything went well, and morale was high. But all of that was to change during the mission two days later.

I've said before that Eugene Calhoun was an excellent navigator, but an aggressive individual. He had gone so far as to boast to me that he and I shared the captaincy of the B-24, implying that I always had to get his approval for major decisions. Teamwork among crew members is important, but everyone knows that the final decision rests with the pilot.

However, I had always been able to overlook, or at least tolerate, Calhoun's arrogance. He and I had always agreed on past missions, but his call on this one could have resulted in our deaths had he had his way. As it happened, we were both successful, and lucky to be alive.

Our last covert mission was on March 28, and we had almost 48 hours before the next one on March 30, so we were well rested by briefing time. It was another mission over Denmark, this time about 10 miles south of Sikebory, a small town about 50 miles east of the North sea.

"We're on course," Calhoun reported as we neared the drop zone. "About ten miles out."

I lowered the flaps, reduced the airspeed, and adjusted our altitude to approximately 500 feet. It was dark, since the lights in Nazi-occupied countries were always blacked out, and Calhoun had to navigate by dead reckoning. We strained our eyes to see the underground fighters at the target area.

Suddenly brilliant flashes of tracer fire lit up the sky in front of us. Pete George sat in the nose of our plane and had the best view of any of us. He screamed, "Turn left fast! Turn left fast!"

I could see the tracers, but George was in a better position to advise me. I immediately made a steep bank to the left. With a heavy load, flaps down, and reduced airspeed, we were a sitting duck for the German guns below.

We found ourselves surrounded by enemy fire. The dense flack and 50 caliber tracers lit up the sky all around us, and we were so low we could hear the explosions of the gunfire. I quickly saw that George had made a mistake. In his excitement he told me to turn left, when he meant for me to watch my left, and turn right. I guided the plane to a 180 heading to escape the gunfire from below.

It took a long minute for us to get on a 180 heading. During that time I wondered what had happened to navigation. Our intelligence was always good, and Calhoun had never strayed before. But it was soon evident that we were 10 miles or more off course.

By now we had escaped the Nazi guns, and I knew exactly where we were. I visualized the map I had studied prior to take-off and figured we were only about three or four minutes away from our target. If we could see the lights from the underground, we would be on a perfect course for a return flight.

I knew everyone was okay except for a rattled Calhoun and George, who were in the nose together. Suddenly, the frantic voice of Calhoun came over the intercom.

"Take a heading of 270 and let's get the hell out of here! George and I are okay, but the nose of the plane is hit!"

"We're almost to the target. I'll stay this course, then take 270 back," I replied.

Calhoun screamed back, "I'm taking control of this plane, Fesmire! I order you to take 270 now!"

"Oh, shut up, Calhoun," I growled back. "We're almost to the target. When we get there, we'll make our drop. Then I'll take 270 back home. Now look sharp, everyone, and look for the target!"

Two minutes later we saw the signal lights. We made the drop, and I turned the plane around to a perfect course for our return flight

"Now we're on 270," I called to Calhoun. He didn't reply, and I wondered how he would take being faced down like that.

The plane had received two hits in the nose, and one had destroyed the navigator's compass. When I learned this, I understood why the men were so frantic. George was scared because a shell had come so close to him. After we made our drop, he made his way to the cockpit and stood quietly between Elliott and me all the way home. Calhoun was frightened for the same reason, and he was embarrassed because we had been several miles off course. Looking back, the rest of us were relatively calm both during and after our encounter.

After we returned home, Calhoun reluctantly admitted that my decisions had been correct during the mission. I was pleased that he had apologized for his actions, and I thanked him. He was an excellent navigator, and I thought he learned who was captain of the plane.

On April 1 Elliott and Calhoun were promoted to first lieutenants. I did not receive my promotion as Colonel St. Clair had promised, and I was pissed off at somebody's idea of a bad

April Fool joke. I had completed 12 missions without an abortion, and the colonel had praised me highly for it. I just couldn't believe it was true.

I really didn't believe that St. Clair had canceled it, but I was still too angry to speak to him about it. Instead, I asked his administrative sergeant if he knew why my promotion was canceled. The sergeant replied that it must have been our group commander who had canceled it.

Great! This was the same guy that had bawled me out for getting my plane stuck in the mud. I figured that he also interpreted my refusal to volunteer for the China assignment as a refusal of an order.

I reluctantly congratulated Calhoun and Elliott on their promotions. I finally told them that I had refused to volunteer for the crew to go to China. They were shocked that I hadn't been promoted, and they were surprised at the China issue. But it didn't matter that much to them, for it was old news.

Calhoun and Elliott were assigned to other crews, and we soon parted company. I wondered what each man thought of our frightful mission over Denmark. This was the last time they would be members of my crew, and it turned out best for me. It was probably best for them, too.[11]

My last covert mission was on March 30, and I learned the next day that my promotion was canceled. But I received some better news on the day after. Colonel St. Clair summoned me to his office. Once again he praised my outstanding combat record, then told me he had good news for me.

I assumed he was going to explain the promotion snafu. Instead he told me that I had been assigned a new copilot and navigator. The new members of my crew and I would go to Lon-

---

11  I rarely saw these men after their promotions and transfers. Calhoun became a navigator on an A-26, and after some transitional training, Elliott became a first pilot. He never got his own crew.

don the next day. We would prepare there for an important operation, then return to base for a thorough briefing. St. Clair assured me that I would be pleased.

I'd be even more pleased with a promotion, I thought, but I held my tongue. I believed he was aware of the cancellation, but he didn't mention it. Nevertheless, his news improved my morale, and I became eager for action once again.

After my conversation with St. Clair, I met my new copilot. John Lancaster had been the regular copilot on Lieutenant Polinsky's crew, but was sick the night of the fatal crash.[12]

The loss of his entire crew affected Lancaster; however, he coped with it effectively, and was an outstanding copilot on my crew.

I also learned that Lancaster was one of St. Clair's favorites. Both of them loved skeet shooting. They participated together in this sport, and Lancaster was one of the best skeet shooters in the Eighth Air Force.

I was very pleased with the navigator who joined our crew. Lieutenant Robert Parks had been a navigator on a bombing crew stationed on the eastern coast of England. He was one of the highest rated navigators in the 8th Air Force. He had completed all of the necessary missions to be eligible for a return to the States, but was engaged to a beautiful English girl and determined to stay in England. He went through a lot of red tape to stay, but he was finally assigned to our Carpetbagger group.

Our crew loosened up when both of these men came aboard. It was apparent that St. Clair was looking out for our best interests, and my respect for the colonel increased.

Lancaster and I boarded a train for London the next morning. It would be a fascinating experience for us. During the train ride

12 There was a rumor that the substitute copilot had bailed out before the crash, but it was never confirmed.

we enjoyed the view of the beautiful English countryside, but as we got closer to London, the scenery became more and more ugly. We saw the craters produced by German bombs. Many buildings lay in shambles, utterly destroyed. But the part that had been hit the worst was the train station. As we rode in we saw a huge hole in the roof.

An American in civilian clothes met us at the station. We boarded an Army van and were taken to a building only a few blocks away from the important government buildings of England. The van took us to our accommodations, where we were briefed by the liaison officer, shown the excellent dining room, then taken to our room for the night. We were to meet him at 9 the next morning at the building's entrance.

As we made our way back to the entrance, we noticed that most of the people coming into the building wore civilian clothes, but they impressed us as important officials. Lancaster and I felt conspicuous in our uniforms, but we were treated like VIPs.

We had some free time before our meeting the next morning, so after lunch in the dining room, we set out to explore London. It was the first time I had been off a military base since coming overseas. We went to Piccadilly Circus, a wild night club area in London where American servicemen on leave gathered. We had walked only a few blocks before some prostitutes approached us.

We amused ourselves by talking to the girls, and we found that, within their price structure, you got what you paid for. The girls who asked for 5 pounds (equivalent to $20 then) were sexier and better dressed, whereas the 2 pound girls were more plain. Some of them explained that they had apartments where you could stay all night if you wished. We thanked them for their time and moved on.

The English had suffered greatly because of the war. Some of these prostitutes made more in one night than they could working at a job for an entire week. I felt sorry for these women who saw no other means of survival.

After leaving the Piccadilly Circus area, we visited Hyde Park. It was beautiful park, but we couldn't see how anyone could relax and enjoy it. Preachers of strange faiths were shouting out their sermons to anyone who would listen.

"Listen to me!" one of them cried. "Listen, all of you! You haven't much time. You must prepare yourselves now, for the earth will soon be destroyed!"

I thought of my father and wondered what he would say were he here. We walked on to London Bridge and toured a few other sights before returning to our hotel.

After dinner, we returned to the Piccadilly Circus area to take in the night life. Every night club and pub around was packed with American servicemen. And for every soldier, there were at least three ladies of the evening trying to ply their trade.

While we were there that evening, I ran into Gerald Wilburn, a Vanderbilt classmate and fellow pole vaulter. He also was a bomber pilot, and we took the chance to catch up on the gossip of our other classmates.

The next morning, a man in plainclothes came into our room at 7:00 and woke us. He told us to get dressed, eat and be ready by 8:30. He also mentioned that Robert Parks, our new navigator, would also be briefed and join us at the Carpetbagger base upon our return.

We met our liaison at 8:30. We walked together to another building where we had passport photographs made in civilian clothes and new passports prepared for Sweden and Russia. After some briefing we climbed aboard a bus that took us to a large warehouse. The interior was filled with civilian clothes, and we were fitted with sport coats, trench coats, and ties. Our liaison then told us that we were free until the next morning, when we were to return to our base.

We rode a double-decker bus around town, then got off in front of a government building. An attractive woman stepped out of the building just as the bus drove away. It was late afternoon, and she had just finished her work for the day. We ran over to talk to her.

She was polite and interested in what we had to say; then she quickly changed the subject.

"You know," she said, "my roommate and I have an apartment nearby. If you need some company and a place to stay, it's yours for five pounds each."

Lancaster and I looked at each other. We were used to women who sold themselves, and obviously we could get whatever we wanted from this girl and her roommate. But what amazed us was that a government worker—someone with a good job—had to sell her body to survive.

"Are you particular with the men you, um, ask over?" I asked her. She laughed.

"Not at all, Yank! I'm happy when any soldier—or soldiers-gives me five pounds in exchange for an evening. Nationality doesn't matter. I've done it with Americans, Frenchmen, Poles, you name it. Race doesn't matter. I've done it with blacks and whites. It's all the same to them, they all do it the same way, so it's all the same to me. Five pounds gets them what they want and pays for what I need."

Her bluntness took me aback, and suddenly I lost all interest, though I really felt sorry for her. From what she said, it was obvious that the entire country was short on everything they needed to live on, and that a black market economy was thriving. What Churchill later said about owing so much to so many was true, but the Allies also owed a tremendous debt to the English for the sacrifices they made to defeat a madman.

Lancaster and I enjoyed our trip to London. I continued to be unhappy because my promotion was canceled; however, I had friendly thoughts toward Colonel St. Clair. I knew he wasn't the one who canceled my promotion.

**Robert Fesmire after having been assigned a crew.
September, 1944.**

**Pilot and Co-pilot
John Lancaster
and
Robert Fesmire**

**John Carnivale
B-24**

**Robert Parks. Metfield Air Transport Command Airfield.**

**Fesmire's Original Crew: (Back row: l-r) Pete George, Ken Elliott, Eugene Calhoun, George Spencer, George Philbrick. (Front row: l-r) Jack Keeley, John Carnevale, George Weitzel, Leonard Kanehl, Bob Fesmire.**

**Robert Fesmire, Douglas, GA. 1943.
PT-17 Primary.**

**BT-13A. Basic plane.**

**PT-17**
**Primary**

**AT-10**
**Advanced**

*Description of bearer*

Height: 6 feet — inches.

Hair: Blonde

Eyes: Grey

Distinguishing marks or features:

Place of birth: Lexington, Tennessee

Date of birth: May 6, 1923

Occupation: Airline official

Robert H. Fesmire

*Signature of bearer.*

This passport is not valid unless signed by the person to whom it has been issued.

3

**Page from Robert Fesmire's passport. Note the line describing "Occupation."**

**Robert Fesmire at his dental practice in Nashville, TN.**

**Williamsburg, 1992.**
**Two old "Carpetbaggers."**
**John Lancaster, Robert Fesmire**

**The Fesmire's at the Dinner**

Veterans of the O.S.S.

1991 Dinner

and presentation of

The William J. Donovan Award

to

The President of the United States

George Bush

Wednesday evening, the twenty-third of October

International Ballroom

The Washington Hilton

Washington, District of Columbia

# 7

# Missions to Sweden

After returning to our Carpetbagger group on April 5, Lieutenant Robert Parks officially became our navigator. It was hard not to contrast his temperament with Calhoun's. Parks was easy to get along with, and I could see that he was team-oriented. In fact, I treated him just like a brother from the moment he joined us. Everyone welcomed the addition of Parks and Lancaster. This was a happy crew, and we were ready for action.

We received more information about the operation in which we were to participate. We were to be temporarily assigned to Metfield Air Transport base, a base in eastern England, and close to the southern part of the North Sea. Our mission was to transport military supplies in containers to Stockholm. We would wear civilian clothes, and each of us would have an official passport showing he was an airline official. This way, we wouldn't violate Sweden's neutrality—at least not officially. Once there, these secret containers of military supplies would be unloaded from our plane and trucked across the border to Norway to be used by Major Colby, his OSS men, and other underground forces.

Lieutenant Parks and I discussed what flight plan we should use in flying to Stockholm. It was obvious that we would have to fly over Nazi-occupied Norway during our flight to Stockholm. We had always been briefed on what to accomplish in a covert mission. Our intelligence officer was always available to give us a map that showed Nazi gun positions. He always gave us accurate information, and Parks and I wondered if we would receive any briefing by the ATC group. These were people with their own ways of doing things.

"What if they send us over German guns?" Parks asked. "We're unarmed, and we'd be a sitting duck."

"Let's hedge our bet," I replied. "Let's go see our intelligence officer before we leave."

I had great confidence in our intelligence people and their agents in occupied countries. Using this reliable information, our intelligence officer decided the most safe and practical path for flying across Norway to arrive at Stockholm. He drew it on a map, and it proved to be a lifesaver, though we didn't know it at the time. We never received any intelligence information from the officials at Metfield prior to any of our Stockholm flights.

On April 9 Robert Parks, John Lancaster, John Carnevale, Jack Keeley, and I made the one hour flight to Metfield ATC. When we arrived, a military van was ready to take us to our barracks. During this short ride we were amazed at the beauty of this airfield. The barracks and all of the buildings were modern stucco structures, and the grounds were beautifully manicured.

Most Air Transport Command pilots stationed here had been civilian pilots with a great deal of flying experience. But the war against Germany was so serious that these pilots had been inducted into the military as officers, though they received little or no military training. Despite this handicap, the ATC pilots gave great service during the war by flying people and supplies to non-combat areas.

The next morning I reported to Colonel Bernt Balchen, the commanding officer at Metfield. I was astonished that he showed an unfriendly attitude toward me. He said as little as he could to me; then another officer took me across the room to take care of other business. It was there where I overheard a remark made by the colonel to the other ATC officers around him.

"I don't know why they sent 8th Air Force crews for this operation," he growled in a heavy Norwegian accent. "Their pilots are no good. Our pilots are much more qualified. It's going to be a failure!"

That pissed me off, and I made sure I would remember his name. His attitude gave me the impression that he didn't give a damn whether we succeeded or not; in fact, it almost seemed that he wanted us to screw up so that he could justify his opinions. I decided to be cautious in following any order given by him.

Our crew was free the next couple of days, so I decided to find out more about the colonel. I approached some of the ATC pilots about Colonel Balchen, and they thought he was great. I learned that he was one of the most famous pilots in the history of aviation, having flown over the South Pole with Admiral Byrd.

He was Norwegian by birth, and he had become an American citizen. From what I could gather from the other ATC pilots, Balchen wanted to be the man responsible for freeing Norway from German occupation. It was a lofty goal, but one entirely fueled by ego. His dream sounded like that of a younger man, and I thought it strange coming from someone who appeared to be 45.

But this love for his native land just inspired him to be more ambitious. He wanted to be promoted to general, and he made sure everyone knew about it. Balchen also resented that OSS was in charge of all Carpetbagger covert operations, and he was convinced that he could do a better job. In fact, he undertook some unauthorized secret missions by himself just to prove that point. He was well-suited for intelligence work, and the OSS could have used him as they had used Major Colby. Balchen spoke English, German, Swedish, and Norwegian (perhaps more). He had his own sources in Norway, and he was enough of a maverick to do the work.

By the time I had talked to two or three pilots, my opinion of the colonel improved. His pilots had great respect for the old codger.

Our crew received a notice to fly our first covert mission to Stockholm on April 12. I expected no briefing, but was still disgusted when one wasn't given. Our only directions were to fly to Stockholm with a planeload of military supplies. We were to take off early that evening. Fortunately, Parks and I had the foresight to consult our Carpetbagger intelligence officer for a flight plan, and we played our ace that night.

Before takeoff we were given our passports, Swedish kronors, and Swedish ration coupons. Our flight to Stockholm was routine, the weather was perfect, and Parks and I took the opportunity to talk about colonels and their relative IQ.

"Chief, did you ever hear of a colonel at Cochran Field in Macon?" he asked.

"Which one?"

"Oh, this one was crazy as hell. Spent time in a psychiatric hospital."

Suddenly I remembered the time that I had been falsely accused of gambling. I remembered the hearing, the fear in the officer's faces, and their concern over keeping the matter quiet.

"Yeah, I knew about him," I replied. "Almost washed me out."

"Well, he did wash me out," Parks said bitterly.

I was stunned. That crazy colonel had taken a perfectly good officer and kept him out of a pilot's seat.

"You know what I'm gonna do when this war's over?" Parks went on. "I'm gonna find that damn colonel and beat the hell out of him!"

I was truly sorry for Parks. He was an excellent navigator, and I was sure he could have been an excellent pilot as well.

We landed at the Broma airport a little after midnight. We put on our sport coats and ties, then reported to the Swedish officials so they could stamp our passports. After this routine we were taken to an apartment complex where we would have a few hours of sleep.

Very early the next morning Parks, Lancaster, and I were ready for sightseeing. We put on our coats and ties, and with our passports we became regular American civilians. Lancaster suggested going to mid-city Stockholm where we could find a restaurant. The ATC group had given us a liberal amount of Swedish money for eating and enough to pay for other limited activities. We also had ration coupons for food.

We ended up in the main area of downtown Stockholm, and I thought it was a beautiful city. The bright sunshine felt good in the cold air. Thousands of bicycles crowded the streets, their riders busily pedaling to work. What few automobiles there were each had a small, 3-foot high stove attached on the side of the hood. It was obvious that there was a fire in the stove, but little or no smoke was coming from it. There was a metal tube from the stove to the engine of the auto, and I realized that the cars had been converted to run off of the hydrocarbon gases produced by the burning fuel. The top speed of these vehicles couldn't have been more than 10 miles per hour.

One car was stalled, and the driver was refueling the stove on his car with what appeared to be coke or a wood product. These automobiles moved very slowly with this inefficient fuel. I reasoned that Sweden had no petroleum production, and gasoline was not available.

After walking around the city for awhile, we found a very nice restaurant. We had our Swedish phrase books, but we didn't have to use them. The waitress could speak and understand English.

Lancaster, Parks, and I enjoyed a late breakfast of reindeer steak, fresh fried eggs, and rolls, and we washed all of it down with lager beer. We learned that the beer was brewed in Nazi

Germany, since the two countries enjoyed normal trade relations.

"It's the only good thing to come out of that country." Lancaster said, raising his mug.

We were at the restaurant during midmorning. The workers hadn't had their lunch breaks yet, and the restaurant was almost empty. There was only one other table with customers, and we couldn't keep from looking at the Oriental men at the table in back of the restaurant.

"Who are those men?" I asked our waitress as she passed.

"I don't know," she replied, "but I think they're Japanese." The men indicated by the waitress watched our actions closely and suddenly began to speak rapidly among themselves. They threw some money on the table and rushed out through the back door.

"Huh!" I snorted when they had gone. "Now what do you make of that?"

"Looks like we scared 'em," Lancaster replied. "They probably thought we were gonna capture and torture 'em."

Parks drank his beer. "Maybe they'll drop dead."

After leaving the restaurant Lancaster and I each bought a Movado calendar watch at a nearby jewelry store. In our conversation with the salesman we learned that he had lived in New York City for six years. He had been unhappy in our country, and he moved back to Sweden. I wondered if he were pro-Nazi, but decided against debating the point with him; besides, I was too proud of the watch. It cost approximately $35, and after the war Life magazine advertised it for $150.

After a busy day we learned that we would fly back to England that night. An electric street car took us back to the vicinity where we had slept after our landing at the Broma airport. During our ride on the streetcar Lancaster, Parks, and I did a lot of talking. Some of the women on the car began listening to us, and one woman with a British accent exclaimed, "These Americans don't know how to speak English!"

Several people laughed loudly, and it was obvious that they were making fun of our accents. We were both amused and irritated. I began to think that some Swedes were pro-German during the war.

As we neared our apartment area we were surrounded by Swedish children. While holding out their hands they yelled, "Gum, chum! Gum, chum!" We didn't have any gum, but we were surprised to hear this begging in Stockholm. It was common in England because American troops were stationed there. But we soon realized that many American bomber crews were interned in Sweden after their planes had been damaged over Germany.

Our flight to Metfield was routine during April 13. While over the North Sea we heard over our plane's radio that President Roosevelt had died. I thought little of the news. My parents were both Republican, and my mother was a charter member of the Ladies Republican Party of Nashville.[13] We embraced their political beliefs, I to the point that I voted against Roosevelt twice in the same election![14]

The ground crew welcomed us home, and we expressed our appreciation to them. After returning from our first covert flight to Stockholm, we gave our passports to a sergeant in the operations office.

"Aren't they going to debrief us?" Lancaster asked me.

I doubted it, but decided to wait around for a while in case someone cared to. Not a single officer approached us for debriefing.

---

13 It's ironic that she was in the GOP in the South at a time when other Southern ladies would call her (of all things) a carpetbagger.

14 My father had mailed me an absentee ballot, I had voted, and mailed it back. In the meantime, he had moved, and he was unsure if I had received the ballot, so he mailed me another. Despite my efforts, Roosevelt still defeated Dewey.

"We always got debriefed," Parks remarked.

"Maybe ATC doesn't give a damn," I replied. "I know Colonel Balchen doesn't." I yawned and stretched. "Well, if they want us they can wake us up. Let's get some sleep."

I had left the barracks with my bunk unmade. When I returned I discovered that my bunk was beautifully made with fresh clean sheets. This was quite a contrast to our Carpetbagger base which furnished only GI blankets. Maybe these ATC guys aren't so bad after all, I thought as I drifted off to sleep.

Later that afternoon our crew made a quick flight to our Carpetbagger base to check on our mail. We enjoyed visiting with our friends there. Two pilots were amazed at my Movado calendar watch, and each one asked me to buy him a watch on our next flight to Stockholm. Some of my friends seemed envious when I described what fun we had.

While I was visiting our Carpetbagger operations area Colonel St. Clair entered the room. We greeted each other, then he remarked, "We're proud of your record, Lieutenant Fesmire. How do you like the operations you're flying?"

I replied, "Thank you, Sir. We enjoy what we are doing very much."

I described our trip to London and told him how much I enjoyed it. I then told him about our exciting day in Stockholm. I was wound up as I continued. He was involved in the conversation and he was pleased that I was happy.

Colonel St. Clair concluded by saying, "Let me know if I can help you in any way."

This was the time!

"Colonel, do you mind if I get something off my chest?" I said abruptly.

St. Clair looked puzzled. "Not at all," he replied. "What's your problem? I'll be glad to help."

I unloaded, and the words seemed to tumble out of me. "You told me during the last week of March that I was being promoted to first lieutenant. Now, my copilot and navigator were promoted, but my promotion was canceled by someone. I don't blame you, but I want to know if you have a first pilot with a better record than mine."

With some shock Colonel St. Clair replied, "I didn't realize your promotion was canceled, Lieutenant. But I want you to know it wasn't my fault. Come into my office and I will take care of it immediately."

A few minutes after I left St. Clair's office, Major Ross White, my operations officer, approached me. He was aware of my conversation with the colonel.

"You were screwed, Lieutenant," he said to me. "But don't worry about it. The colonel will take care of your promotion to first lieutenant, and when that comes through, I'll put you up for captain."

I made sure I expressed appreciation to both St. Clair and White. I respected both men, and on this day my morale jumped sky-high. The only unpleasant thought in my mind was realizing that the famous colonel at Metfield had made me feel unwelcome, and that I still had to work for him for a while. But this didn't stop me from enjoying the visit to home base.

Lieutenant Parks, our navigator, didn't make the trip with us when we visited our Carpetbagger base. During this time he enjoyed being with his beautiful English fiancee, and he considered himself lucky to be stationed so near her home.

The next morning as Lancaster and I were walking to the mess hall for breakfast, we looked up to see approximately twenty B-17 bombers maneuvering into formations. The planes were approximately two miles away, and it was a beautiful sight. We watched as two B-17s approached each other to get in wing-to-wing positions. Bombers always fly close together when in formation, but these two maneuvered too close to each other.

Suddenly, their wings locked together, and before we knew what was happening, both planes were in slow spins, diving straight down to the ground. They crashed with tremendous force, and there was a loud explosion as the fuel tanks burst into flames. No one had the chance to bail out, and it was obvious that all crew members in both planes were killed.

It was an emotional sight for Lancaster, and it showed long after the event. He had enough trouble talking about his first crew without getting upset, and I'm sure this crash made him relive the night his crew perished in northern Scotland during a mission to drop OSS men and supplies to support Major Colby's operation. Lancaster was alive because he was sick that night and did not fly with his crew.

# 8

# Second Flight to Stockholm

During late afternoon on April 16 we were getting ready to fly our next covert mission to Stockholm. The experience was similar to what happened before our take-off on the previous mission: Colonel Balchen had a sour expression on his face, and we received no briefing.

Again we followed the flight plan which we had received from our Carpetbagger intelligence officer, and we had a routine flight to the Broma airport in Stockholm. On our arrival our liaison officer notified Lancaster, Parks, and me that we would have rooms in the best hotel in downtown Stockholm, and when we arrived we saw that the officer wasn't kidding. The lobby was decorated with elaborate statuary and paintings, and the rooms were extra large and equipped with private baths. This twenty-one year old from Tennessee felt like a VIP.

Lancaster, Parks and I left the hotel after a few hours of sleep. After enjoying sight-seeing, we found a fancy restaurant where we decided to eat. A waitress who spoke English led us to an area toward the rear of the restaurant.

We were the only ones in that area of the restaurant aside from a table of men close by. They were talking and laughing, and although I didn't recognize the language, I thought I recognized a face. As I sat down I stared at the man, trying to place where I had seen him. He stared back, and I did what any Southerner would do in such a case: I waved and gave him a friendly smile.

Suddenly the men got quiet and began to whisper among themselves. Within a minute they left the restaurant in a rush, and it was obvious that they didn't finish eating. As the man turned away I suddenly realized who he was.

*I've just publicly acknowledged a leader of the Danish underground!*

He was the same man who had visited our Carpetbagger base a few days after we encountered so much enemy fire over Copenhagen. The gentleman had spoken during the latter part of March, and I had listened to his discussion of the success of Denmark's underground war against Germany. Even though he couldn't say much, we gained a greater understanding of the big picture from his remarks.

But he had to live with caution while in Stockholm. The Germans would love to kill him, and I had possibly helped the enemy. I regretted what happened, but could do nothing about it. My only excuses were my youth and lack of OSS training. At my young age I had no thoughts of caution.

During our earlier sight-seeing we had passed a theater, and we went back to watch the feature. The American movie we saw was average, and the German news reel was a joke. We couldn't understand the language, but there were English subtitles. Germany was winning the war. The Russians were retreating, and Allied armies were in a stalemate. It was like a cartoon to us. We laughed a lot, and we wondered how anyone could believe this propaganda.

A van took us back to Broma during early evening. After arriving at the airport I headed for the Operations Office to file a flight plan. The door to the office was partly closed, and I opened it, only to make my second espionage-related faux pas of the day.

Two men in flight suits were talking and laughing with two Swedish operations officers. I thought that the airmen were Swedish pilots, so I made a friendly gesture and spoke to them.

Suddenly one of the operations officers came over, grabbed me by the arm, and forced me out of the room.

"What do you think you're doing?" he hissed, barely able to control his disgust and anger. "Those men in there are German pilots!"

"I'm sorry, Sir, I had no idea, but ..."

"Look," he went on, "I'll give you some good advice that may save your life one day. If you're an American, don't open a closed door while in Stockholm."

I didn't dare tell the Swede that he couldn't have been too concerned since the door was half open. Nor did I voice my opinion of a so-called "neutral" country where many citizens had been pro-German at the beginning of the war, but had switched their position once the Nazis began losing. I suspected the operations officers still favored Germany.

I walked away from the office. I had not been trained in OSS-style operations, I mused, but I've always been successful in combat operations. I was irritated, thinking I should have told the Swede to try and argue with success.

After finally receiving a flight plan, our crew took off from the Broma airport after dark on April 17. We flew through the night and arrived at Metfield after dawn. Our Carpetbagger flight plan had been perfect during the two round-trip flights. Once again there was no ATC debriefing, and we were ready to sleep.

A few days after our second Stockholm flight, an ATC captain was in front of me in the chow line at the officers' mess hall.

"Serve up that steak, private," he said, pointing to a beautiful T-bone.

"Sorry, Sir," the private replied as he handed over another steak.

"What do you mean, 'sorry, sir'? I order you to give me that steak!"

The private looked at the ATC captain and pointed to my 8th Air Force patch.

"Captain, this man behind you is a combat pilot," the private explained. "He gets the best steak."

This was all very unusual, and I kept quiet. I felt sorry for the captain, but I wasn't going to argue with the private if he wanted to give me the best he had. My only regret was that it wasn't Colonel Balchen in front of me.

Our crew enjoyed the six days of relaxation after returning from Stockholm. Lieutenant Parks especially enjoyed the time off, since he was able to be with his English fiancee. Our missions to Stockholm were going well enough, and we assumed that Major Colby and his OSS men had received the military supplies.

# 9

# Third Mission to Stockholm

On April 23, our crew was notified that we would fly our third covert mission to Stockholm, and I was surprised when I received an order to report directly to Colonel Balchen. We had received no ATC preflight instructions on previous missions, and I wondered why he thought he should start now. Needless to say, I was apprehensive.

On reporting to the colonel I saluted him with proper military courtesy. Unlike Colonel St. Clair or our Carpetbagger intelligence officer, Balchen did not commend our crew for our two successful covert flights over Nazi-occupied Norway. Instead, he got straight to the point.

"Lieutenant Fesmire, we have not liked your flight plans to and from Stockholm. Your flights are too short for what we expect during wartime conditions, and the hours in your logs indicate that your paths over Norway are foolish. I am giving you a flight plan prepared by me, and I order you to use it."

You mean you don't like our intelligence officer's flight plan, I thought.

"Yes, Sir!" I replied. I accepted the flight plan, saluted, and left.

This would be the most unpleasant flight I would experience throughout my military service. We entered bad weather within minutes after takeoff, and it stayed with us throughout the trip. There was cloud cover all the way to Stockholm, and Parks couldn't see any stars to aid him in navigation. Nor was he sure of the velocity and direction of the wind, both of which had a great effect on the heading of our B-24. None of us could see any landmarks on the ground.

We were flying at 180 miles per hour, and we were blind as a bat.

Parks had to work diligently for nine hours in a calculated guess, using dead reckoning, the compass, and divine guidance to determine our plane's position. That night he proved himself an excellent navigator. He saved us from disaster.

In using Balchen's flight plan we approached the Arctic Circle, and the night air was cold as we took an eastern heading over Norway to reach Sweden. We were in the clouds over a mountainous area halfway across Norway. Suddenly our black B-24 was lit up with blue-white beams of light from bright sparks inside and outside of the plane. The four propellers displayed big circles of sparkling brightness. This unusual occurrence resembled a massive Fourth of July display, and it lasted approximately fifteen minutes.

At first all of us were scared, but after a few minutes we realized the bright sparks were discharges of static electricity which would cause no harm. (After we returned to Metfield, I learned from ATC pilots that these sparks were called St. Elmo's Fire. This phenomenon would show up under the right temperature and humidity conditions.)

After almost nine hours in the clouds with Colonel Balchen's flight plan, Parks spoke up.

"I think we're somewhere near Stockholm, Chief," he reported. "But this soup's been so thick we could be over New York."

"How much fuel?" I asked Keeley, our flight engineer. "Low. Real low. We need to land fast."

I tried to raise Broma's control tower but got no answer. I flew the B-24 in a circle while John Carnevale tried to make radio contact. Carnevale was an excellent radio operator, and I was surprised he received no answer.

"Chief," Keeley said, "we've gotta land now!"

"How much time?"

"Ten minutes, maybe."

Because of Balchen's flight plan our B-24 was almost out of gas. We kept trying to get a radio compass heading to Broma airport with a radio transmission from the control tower, but they still refused to answer. I sweated out a couple of long minutes, then made a decision.

"Damn Swedes," I grunted as I reached for the radio microphone, hoping I was on the correct frequency.

"Broma, we are in the clouds. We need your transmission for a radio compass heading. If you don't give us transmission, we are going to open our bomb bays and drop a load!"

I wondered if they received my threat. Carnevale had worked fast as lightning to get a response from Broma, and he should get the credit for a successful communication.

We received cooperation from the control tower, and with a radio compass heading we saw the lights from the Broma airport within a few minutes. It was ironic that the airport had a five mile radius of clear sky above after we had flown nine hours in the clouds.

I requested and received landing instructions, and I was careful to thank the Swede for giving us a long enough radio transmission to get a heading to the airport. It was doubtful that I would thank Colonel Balchen for his "superior" flight plan.

Lancaster, Parks, and I enjoyed the luxury of separate rooms in the downtown hotel. We had landed at Broma airport just before daylight. Although we were exhausted from the long and stressful flight, we got up early. After the few hours of sleep we were ready for activity.

I had shown my Movado calendar watch to friends during a recent visit to our Carpetbagger base, and I remembered that they wanted watches, too. So after eating breakfast I asked Lancaster and Parks to go with me to the nearby jewelry store where I had bought my watch.

The store had two watches left, though the price would cost me the greater part of my expense money. I hated to spend most of my Swedish kroners, but there was a solution in the form of two $20 bills in my wallet.

"I can't accept American money," the salesman said when I pulled the bills out.

"Why not?" I asked. "It's good U.S. cash."

"I can't," he insisted. "But you can exchange your money for kronor's at the bank across the street. It will not take long."

That sounded like a good idea to me, and Lancaster and Parks agreed to wait for me while I made a trip to the bank.

The first man I approached spoke English, and I asked him to please exchange my American currency for Swedish money.

The Swede replied, "Wait here, please."

Within a few minutes a Swedish policeman was on either side of me, and I was threatened with arrest. They walked me to the American Embassy three blocks away.

The American official in charge of such matters greeted me. "Welcome to Sweden," he said. "Now what are you trying to do?"

I showed him my passport and explained that I was an airline pilot. He read every word of the document. Then he scrutinized the money.

"You realize that you're not supposed to have U. S. currency here in Sweden," he said at last.

I knew it was against military policy to have U.S. money overseas, but I couldn't let him know I was military, so I played dumb.

"No, Sir, I didn't," I replied. "I'm sorry. It's just that a couple of my friends wanted those watches."

He glanced over my passport once more before handing it back to me. "I'm sorry that you were detained," he said, "but it was a necessary precaution on our part. There is a lot of counterfeit American money in Sweden—elsewhere too, for that matter—and the banker thought your bills were fake."

"I'm sorry," I repeated. "It won't happen again."

"Next time, exchange your money before you come," he replied. "But for now I can help you out."

The American official exchanged my forty dollars for an equivalent amount in kronors. I thanked him, and he wished the best for me.

Parks and Lancaster had worried about me, but I finally returned to the jewelry store. They were amused by my story and my being at the American embassy. I bought two Movado calendar watches for my friends at our Carpetbagger base, then left.

Parks, Lancaster, and I enjoyed walking around mid-city Stockholm. It was a beautiful day, and at noon the sidewalks were crowded. Several restaurants had tables on the sidewalks so working people could eat and enjoy the sunshine. We wished we could spend several weeks in Stockholm enjoying the weather, food, and the beautiful Swedish girls.

Later in the afternoon I learned that the Germans had set off a bomb in the U.S. Embassy where I had been not two hours ago. No American official received an injury, but it gave me an eerie feeling.

On our previous mission to Stockholm we saw several American P-51 fighter planes put on a show. The pilots, flying in formation, buzzed the city from a few hundred feet above the ground, then continued with a great exhibition of acrobatic maneuvers.

Our crew had been in a great position to witness the show of our P-51s, but we did not see one act of their performance. The show ended with a game of follow the leader as the leader flew under a bridge in the city. We learned that the Swedish government had made a strong protest concerning these acrobatic flights. The Swedes were especially upset because they flew under the bridge.

We learned that our government had made a gift of the P-51s to Sweden. Our pilots had flown the fighters to Stockholm, and they wanted to show off their skill. I had firsthand knowledge about how good these hotshot pilots were. At the ATC base, I had watched in amazement as a P-51 flew under an electrical line that hung about 100 feet off the ground.

During our third visit to Stockholm we became aware that the attitudes of Swedes toward America had changed. Many of them were angry over the performance of our P-51 pilots, and whenever we talked to them, they complained about the flights under the bridge. They knew we were Americans, and some Swedes were not as friendly as they were during our previous trips to Stockholm.

During mid-afternoon Parks, Lancaster, and I entered a bar. We had drunk plenty of Scotch whiskey during the last few months in England. Since we were in Stockholm we decided to experiment with other types of liquor. After trying schnapps we had two drinks of Russian vodka. We quit barely in time because we had to be sober for a long flight to England.

Soon after leaving the bar an American liaison gentleman took us to the Broma airport. Our return flight to England was delayed because of a change in the weather. We had a long time to sober up and to think about Balchen's flight plan that had brought us to Stockholm.

"Fellas, I think it would be a mistake to use the colonel's plan again," I said. "It was bad enough the first time."

Parks nodded. "We barely made it with a full load. The bomb bays will be empty going back, and we'll be lighter, but we'll be fighting west winds."

"So the difference is about the same," Lancaster said. "How much time will the other flight plan save?"

"Three hours." Parks paused, then added, "Of course, if we use the old one, there's the chance that the gun markings are no longer accurate." "And if Balchen finds out, we could be court martialed," Lancaster said.

"So we could possibly run into German gunfire or definitely run out of gas over the North Sea," I said. "That's an easy decision. I say if everybody's comfortable with it, to hell with the colonel!"

Everyone else agreed. We had little fear of facing Colonel Balchen after our landing at Metfield.

As it turned out, there was no enemy fire, and our six hour return trip to the ATC base was a joy ride compared to the frightening nine hour flight to Stockholm. Our only worry was that Balchen would learn that we did not use his flight plan.

Soon after our landing at Metfield I became very angry. I was standing on the ramp close to our B-24 when a short, silly looking Englishman approached me.

"Good day, gentlemen," he said. "I trust you had an enjoyable visit in Stockholm."

I looked at Lancaster and tried not to laugh.

"We sure did," I replied.

"Lovely city. So many beautiful hotels, restaurants, women. And such charming shops! Tell me, did you happen to buy some nice things while you were there?"

I showed him the two Movado watches I had bought. The other crew members did not respond.

"Excellent choices," he said. "Of course you realize you'll have to pay eight pounds import tax. You see, I'm with the British Customs Office."

I looked at the man, and got the sudden feeling that I was being conned.

"What's that in American money?" I asked.

"Oh, about $32."

I was furious! The total cost of the watches was already $70, and this limey wanted to jack up the price to over a hundred. I pointed out that I was fighting a war for his country and mine. He pointed out that he was just doing his job, and we argued back and forth. Finally this maverick decided to fall back on his philosophy of avoiding fights you can't win.

"We're flying back to Stockholm tonight," I lied, "and I'll take the watches back and get a refund."

I walked away from the customs officer, and our crew headed for the barracks. I was in no mood to confront Colonel Balchen. We kept our passports, and we did not receive a debriefing.

Around noon, a greatly concerned ATC captain came into our barracks. We had not reported to the ATC operations office after our landing, he told me. (We never had to before, I thought.) Metfield officers were afraid that we were missing-in-action. The captain was so glad that we were alive that he didn't mention the passports. I was relieved that I had avoided Colonel Balchen.

That damn English customs officer came into the barracks the next morning and again demanded eight pounds in tax for the two Movado watches. He had learned that I did not fly to Stockholm during the previous night, and by now I knew he was a con artist. But I was irritated beyond measure by now, and I decided to throw my weight around.

"Who in the hell are you?" I roared at the silly-looking man. "I've never seen you before!"

The customs officer tried to respond, but I interrupted. "Get out of here! I don't know what you're talking about!"

He practically ran out through the door, and I never saw or heard of him again. All I knew was that I wasn't going to pay

$32 dollars in tax for a $70 purchase, and that something was wrong with the customs officer.

After our last mission to Stockholm we had the equivalent of a vacation at the Metfield Air Transport Command base. We were housed in a modern barracks, and we had maid-type service. Sleeping between clean sheets was a luxury compared to the dirty blankets we had to use at our Carpetbagger base. What's more, the ATC base had a beautiful officer's club. I played a lot of bridge there during the last week of April. Lancaster, Parks, and I lived it up at the bar and the mess hall with their excellent food. But the greatest joy I had was knowing I would never be confronted by Colonel Balchen again.

The end of the war was approaching when we received orders to report to our home base. I felt like I was returning to the base with a good crew, although we had to say good-bye to Parks in early May. He had requested and received permission to be permanently stationed near his girlfriend. I was disappointed to lose such a fine man and navigator. But Lancaster would remain with us, and I knew I would want to be the pilot of this crew under any combat situation.

While I was collecting my things I made sure to pack my civilian clothes and passport. I knew I was supposed to return the passport to Colonel Balchen, but I decided that it would be a meaningful souvenir for years to come. Besides that, it gave me great satisfaction to know that I had disobeyed even this small order of his.

When I was ready to leave the barracks for the flight to our Carpetbagger base, I noticed a stack of clean sheets. I knew these sheets were not available at my home base, and I felt I had as much right to them as the ATC officers. So I packed a stack of them in a barracks bag and took them with me. Equipped with the pilfered laundry, I was ready for our return flight home.

As soon as our plane was airborne, I suddenly had a wicked thought. Our B-24 was a few feet above the runway when I saw the control tower at 10 o'clock in front of us. I banked our plane left and headed directly for it, pulling up just in time to miss the tower, then continuing on our course toward home.

Sergeant Carnevale, our radio operator, looked at me with wide eyes.

"Chief, you realize how close we came to the tower?" he said.

"Yeah," I replied. "Maybe it'll show him how we felt flying in to Stockholm on fumes from the gas tanks."

"He really hates the 8th Air Force that much?"

"He sure does, and from what I understand, they don't know what to do with him. I'm just glad he's not my problem."

Of course, I could have been court-martialed for buzzing the tower like that, but at the time I didn't care. I just wanted a small measure of revenge.

After landing at our home base, we had a friendly visit with Colonel St. Clair and Major White. I thanked them for the exciting experiences during our Stockholm operations. Major White assured me that I would soon be promoted to captain.

I briefly had my doubts about that promotion when two days later I received a notice to report to Colonel St. Clair. I knew something was wrong when I saw the serious expression on his face.

"Lieutenant Fesmire, I've received word from Colonel Balchen that you endangered many lives by buzzing his control tower. He demands your court martial, and I want an explanation."

I looked St. Clair in the eye. "Sir, the colonel badmouthed the Eighth Air Force pilots and crews. He said that we were young, inexperienced, and ill-qualified for Stockholm flights. He said that his experienced ATC pilots should be flying the missions to Stockholm. He never briefed us, never cooperated with us. And he endangered our lives by making us follow a flight plan that used up too much of our fuel. No thanks to him, we still flew three successful missions to Stockholm.

"As I took off from Metfield, I wanted to show my disrespect. Buzzing the tower was a sudden impulse. I know I shouldn't have done it, and I'm sorry, Sir."

St. Clair surprised me by breaking into a grin. He told me that he didn't blame me for doing it, and said that Balchen's arrogance was well-known throughout the Eighth Air Force.

"I'm proud of your record, Lieutenant," he concluded, "and just between us, this control tower incident won't appear on it." Grateful and relieved, I left his office.

The war against Hitler ended on May 7, 1945, one day after my twenty-second birthday. We cheered when we heard the announcement, but speculation soon began to spread that we would be transferred to China to fly missions against the Japanese. During the following weeks we were happy, but tense and unruly.

# 10

# Post War Activity

During the middle of June, Lieutenant Wilson and I volunteered for a special operation in Paris. Our mission was to fly important personnel back and forth between Paris and Wiesbaden, Germany. Both cities were important headquarters for the Allied leaders.

While flying a C-47 over the English Channel, we thought about all of the sightseeing we could do after we landed. After checking in with the American Command in Paris, we were given rooms in one of the nicer hotels in the city, and we were free for the rest of the day. We saw the Eiffel Tower, the Arc de Triomphe, the Seine River, and several famous buildings. I was amazed at the contrast between Paris and London. The City of Lights had been spared the bombings London had suffered.

It was late afternoon when a young girl approached us. "Hi, monsieur," she said. "You sleep with me?"

By now I had the routine down to an art.

"How much it cost?" I asked.

"Five hundred francs, monsieur."

I decided to dicker with her.

"Too much." I pointed to my fellow pilot. "Five hundred for both of us."

The girl looked horrified. "Monsieur, no! Five hundred francs for just you."

We argued a bit until she became hysterical.

"No, no, monsieur! Zig-zig here! Zig-zig there! Zig-zig all night! You kill me!"

We laughed and waved good-bye, but still I felt sorry for the mademoiselle, having to zig-zig with Germans, Frenchmen, and Americans just to make enough money to eat.

We then decided to go to the famous "Pig Alley", a wild night club area in Paris, just to say we had been there. We hadn't quite gotten there when suddenly a Frenchman in his mid thirties approached us.

"Excuse me, gentlemen," he said in excellent English, "but it appears that you're newly arrived in Paris. I offer my services to you as a guide and translator."

Neither Wilson nor I knew anything about Paris or the language spoken there, so we agreed. We resumed our walk down the sidewalk with our new guide.

Suddenly the Frenchman looked back and broke into a run. We turned and saw a truck loaded with men race past him. It skidded to a stop ahead of him, and several of the men jumped out and cut him off. We turned, looking for a way out ourselves, only to find that we were all surrounded by strange, angry men.

The guide quickly ran back to us. He got between us and held us as tightly as he could. The men struggled with us and yanked the guide away.

One of the Frenchmen pulled the guide to the ground and struck him in the head over and over, until his skull was a concave, bloody mess. When he was satisfied the man was dead, he motioned to his comrades, who quickly threw the body into the truck. The other men climbed in after their cargo, while the leader approached us.

"My apologies, messieurs," he said casually, as though he were apologizing for an untidy room in a hotel. "I am with the French Resistance forces. My men and I have been looking for this... this quisling for weeks."

"Quisling?" I asked.

"A traitor, monsieur," the man holding the bloody club replied. "Vidkun Quisling was once a great leader of Norway, and a friend to Adolf Hitler. But when Hitler began his war, Quisling betrayed his people by handing Norway over to him without a fight." His voice became more bitter. "A traitor, monsieur."

I nodded, thinking of all the brave resistance fighters in Norway our missions had supplied.

"At any rate," he went on, "we are sorry if you were injured or upset by this incident. But we had to prevent his escape at all costs. You are military men. I'm sure you will understand."

He ran back to his comrades in the truck, and it sped away.

The explanation made us feel a little better, and we soon stopped shaking. As we made our way back to our rooms, I mused out loud, "Think this will count as a combat mission?"

I slept well, despite the previous night's events. I was awakened early the next morning for a flight to Wiesbaden. We took off from Orly airport with a group of high-ranking officers.

During our flight, I stared in wonder at the bomb craters that now punctuated Germany's landscape. I knew the explosive force of some of the bombs the Allies had dropped, and I imagined that some of these craters would be around for many years.

After our passengers got off, we took on a general and his aide, an attractive WAC captain. We made small talk, and things were going well until mid-flight.

"I have to go to the bathroom, Lieutenant," the captain said, her voice barely controlling her desperation.

I tried not to smile.

"Well, the only thing I know for you to do is to use the relief tube," I replied.

"Where's that?"

"Behind my seat."

There was a pause as she examined the device. It had a simple cone-shape opening connected to a tube, which carried the waste outside of the plane. Naturally it posed no problem for males.

"I can't use that!" she finally sputtered.

"Well, ma'am," I replied, "there's not much else to do except wait until we land, and that'll be a while."

She thought it over.

"Promise not to look?" she asked at length.

"Promise."

I stared hard at my instruments, at the terrain, at anything, all the while pretending that I couldn't hear the rustle of skirts close by, and that there really wasn't some woman relieving herself right behind me. But when I finally thought she was finished, I couldn't help breaking the silence.

"I'm peeking!"

"Oooohhh, damn!"

"What's the matter?"

"You made me wet myself!"

Suddenly the general burst out laughing, and except for the captain, we all relaxed. It was nice to know that even a general could be as human as the rest of us.

Later that afternoon we ate at a swanky hotel in the middle of Paris, once again enjoying VIP treatment in an elegant dining room.

"So," I began, turning to Wilson. "Are you feeling lucky?"

"What do you mean?" he asked.

"Do you want to try and take in Pig Alley tonight?"

He thought briefly.

"Not really," he finally replied.

"Good. Me neither."

We wound up at a night club in the nicer part of town. While sipping our drinks, an attractive girl approached our table. She had a rose in her hand, and she began to dance provocatively in front of Wilson, then me. As she moved, she slid the rose between her breasts and under her low-cut dress. The more she wiggled, the further it dropped, until it was obviously below her waist.

"Où est la rose?" she asked, leaning closer to us.

We laughed, not understanding.

"Où est la rose?" She indicated the rose. "Monsieur, you can get it, okay?"

We laughed even more, but shook our heads. "No, no!"

She smiled, pulled the rose from between her legs, and waved it in front of our faces. She then sat down at our table, much to our irritation.

Just then, two American paratrooper captains passed our table. They were big and tough-looking. Our unwelcome mademoiselle reached out to grab one of their arms, then suddenly blurted, "Are you queer?"

The captain whirled to face me. "Did you put her up to that?" he demanded.

I could only stare at his collection of combat ribbons as I replied, "No, Sir! She sat down at this table just before you came up."

The paratrooper then drew back his fist and punched the girl on the side of the head, lifting her from the chair. She landed on the floor a few feet away. I thought back to the man who had been beaten to death before my eyes just last night, and figured this girl was dead, too.

Everyone else in the room acted as if nothing had happened. Finally, the mademoiselle stirred into consciousness, though no one moved to help her. Eventually she picked herself up and wobbled outside.

We took that as a cue to leave. We had enjoyed Paris, but the violence of the past two nights had us feeling burned out. We decided to go back to the hotel.

On our way back, we saw a large crowd of formally dressed people standing outside the entrance of another hotel. Curious, we walked over. A party was going on inside an elaborate ball-room filled with American civilians, high-ranking officers, and beautiful women. We decided they needed our company, too, and crashed the party.

A distinguished looking civilian approached us. From his first words I knew he was both Southern and heavily intoxicated. He introduced himself as a congressman from Tennessee. I gave him my name, and told him I was from his home state.

" 'S right? No foolin'?" he drawled, his accent thickened by the alcohol.

"That's right," I assured him.

He hugged me, then led me around to face a large group of people.

"Hey, y'all. Got me a Rebel Eighth Air Force pilot from Tenn'see. He 'n his buddy gonna join our party!"

The really embarrassing part was that this congressman knew my father was a Methodist minister in middle Tennessee, and that caused me to be even more ashamed of his behavior. But this feeling quickly turned to pure disgust when I learned that he was here to evaluate post-war political problems and getting smashed at the taxpayer's expense.

Suddenly I felt him thrust something into my hands.

"You take my key," he said. "Get yourself one of these French broads. Take 'er up there and live it up!"

I stared at him.

"Aw, come on, now. Servicem'n like you's gotta have some fun. Ya'll liberated this country—hell, let her thank you! Besides, I got to keep my constituents happy, and this is the best way I know—know what I mean?"

He winked at me and laughed loudly at his own joke. I pressed the key back into his hands, telling him that I had an early flight the next morning, and that I needed a clear head.

"Oh. I get it. Well, how 'bout 'nother time?"

"Of course, congressman. Another time."

And with that, we left.

I reflected on the congressman's behavior as we walked back to our hotel. I felt nothing less than disgust and contempt for him, and I would remember him for the rest of my life. I was delighted when he lost the next election.

The next morning we flew back to our Carpetbagger base at Harrington. I made sure to thank Colonel St. Clair and Major White enough for allowing me to serve in the Paris operation.

It was early afternoon when I returned to my hut to find a surprise waiting for me. Several other Carpetbaggers surrounded a female as she rhythmically stripped off her clothing. They cheered and clapped as she flung her blouse, bra, and panties into the crowd. I recognized her as a young French refugee who had come to England when her country was occupied. She was a frequent guest at our base, and from the looks of things, I gathered she had spent the night here with one of the pilots.

I walked into my private room which is reserved for the hut leader. My bed was in disarray, my beautiful stolen sheets soiled from the previous evening's activities. Fortunately, I had appropriated more than one set, so I quickly changed the bed.

I returned to the main room in the hut. One of the guys saw a pair of bathing trunks that belonged to Wilson, who was absent at the moment. He threw them to the girl, and she put them on. Just then, Wilson walked in and saw her wearing his trunks. He became angry and insisted she take them off. She did, but that only produced more yells.

"Get her out!" he screamed. "I want that bitch out of this room right now!" A few of the guys ushered her out, her clothes in her hands. Wilson took the soiled trunks and threw them in the trash.

The China question had not gone away, and we still wondered if we would eventually wind up there. Some of our crews had already been transferred to China, and my mind turned to the more pleasant thought of discharge and taking some time off.

I had been so busy in our combat operations that I had not been off base to see the English countryside. Transportation to Kettering was available, and I decided to make the trip. Unfortunately, it was dark when I arrived, so sightseeing was out until morning. I went to a nearby pub, which was about the only thing open.

I was drinking a beer when an attractive, sexy English girl came up and joined me. The first thing I noticed was her beautiful smile, and I marveled that someone in this malnourished country still had such perfect teeth. The next thing I noticed was her aggressiveness. Within minutes I found myself agreeing to go to her apartment. We left the pub and walked a block to a telephone booth.

"Listen, Yank," she said. "Wait here. I have to call ahead to make sure the coast is clear."

She walked off to the booth. I looked around and saw no one. The coast is clear here, I mused. Why not do it right in the booth?

I followed her inside and put my arms around her. She turned around, and I kissed her hard—too hard, I guess, for she quickly pulled away.

"Ow, Yank, you've knocked my teeth loose!"

I drew back, disgusted. False teeth! No wonder her teeth were so perfect! That turned me off more than a cold outdoor shower in the middle of winter. I rushed out of the phone booth and back to the pub. I had been up to the plate more times than I could remember and had struck out each time. Cheer up, Fesmire, I told myself. At least you're consistent.

Our 856th flying personnel and most of the ground crew left our Carpetbagger base for the States during mid-July, 1945, and our plane had several high-ranking officers as passengers. The first leg of our flight took us to Iceland, then to Goose Bay, Labrador. After refueling we flew to Bradley Field in Connecticut. All of us were thrilled to be back in the United States. I looked forward to two weeks leave with my parents, sisters, and brother. My other brothers were still in service.

After visiting with my family for a few days, I drove to the Vanderbilt University campus. I hoped to re-enter the first Monday in September. While I had enjoyed my experiences as a pilot, I was eager to get on with life in peacetime, and I tried to figure out a way to get discharged.

The war against Japan officially ended on August 14, 1945. The next day I went back to the campus to remind Dean Lewis that I would return for the fall quarter, though I still hadn't applied for a discharge.

After finishing my leave with my family and friends, I took a train to Sioux Falls, South Dakota, where I joined my crew. We were happy to see each other, but my main thoughts were to get out of the service. A few days later I had an idea.

I went to the base headquarters to verify the mailing address of the Eighth Air Force commander, General James Doolittle. Next, I wrote a letter asking for an immediate discharge so that I could resume my studies. I reminded him that I had volunteered for service in the Army Air Corps after two years at Vanderbilt. I also reminded him of my excellent combat record, and requested verification of it through Colonel St. Clair. I closed it by assuring the general that I took great pride in serving my country.

Of course, it was a long shot. No doubt the general's office received hard luck stories by the score, each pleading for a discharge. But I had to try.

A few days later a messenger came to my barracks.

"Pack up your gear fast," he said. "Got orders for you to be flown to Atlanta to be discharged."

I could hardly believe it! I didn't even have the time to say good-bye to my crew. We rushed to the airfield, and I boarded a C-47. I was the only passenger on the huge plane during the entire trip to Atlanta, and I sat up front in the cockpit and, for a change, enjoyed the ride without having to make decisions. A commanding general can be good hearted, I mused as I stared out the window.

I received a rapid discharge at Fort Oglethorpe, Georgia, and one of the greatest thrills of my life was coming back to Tennessee. I was quickly re-enrolled at Vanderbilt University, and began the process of readjusting to civilian life.

# 11

# Fifty Years Later

My story of the secret war the Carpetbaggers fought 50 years ago would not be complete unless I brought the reader up to date on what has happened to everybody that served on my crew. But before I mention each one, I will say this about all of them: if future generations have the characteristics these men possessed, our country will continue to be the best place in the world in which to live.

The skill of Sergeant John Carnevale, our radio operator for all eighteen of our missions, was a tremendous contribution to our success in combat. He was an outstanding crewman, and I was not at all surprised to learn that John had transferred his success in the military to the civilian world. He became a businessman after the war, and he and his wife Alice spend their summers in Dracut, Massachusetts. Their winter home is in Hallondale, Florida.

Sergeant Jack Keeley was also with us for every mission, and he was the best flight engineer any crew could have. It was his job to keep the ancient B-24 in working order while we were in the air. After his return, he, his wife, Clara, and their family spent many happy years in Dorchester, Massachusetts. It saddened me to learn that Jack died in 1990.

Our dispatcher, Sergeant George Philbrick, flew twelve missions, and it was his job to make sure Major Colby and his men jumped from our plane in a timely fashion. After the war he married Joyce, his girlfriend before the war, and they now live in Fort Fairfield, Maine. George's venture into the world of business brought him a great deal of success, and he and Joyce look forward each year to their annual ocean cruise.

Lieutenant Kenneth Elliott, my original copilot, flew on twelve missions, including the one to drop Colby and his men over Norway. After he left the service, Ken became a successful engineer, and is happily married with a family. I thoroughly enjoyed my time in the service with this fine man.

Lieutenant Eugene Calhoun was my original navigator and flew eleven Carpetbagger missions with us. He always worked at being the best at everything he did, and it came as no surprise to me when I learned of his successful law practice in Madison, Wisconsin. He also became a colonel in the Air Force Reserves, and was a head football official in the Big Ten Football Conference.

Peter George, our original bombardier, flew eleven of our eighteen missions, and he was an excellent crew member. He lives in Masury, Ohio, and his greatest enjoyment is being with his grandchildren. He always hit the drop area.

Lieutenant Robert Parks lives in McDonald, Pennsylvania. He had flown the required number of combat missions to return to the United States, but elected to remain in England because of his beautiful Irish girlfriend. He and Molly were married soon after the war. Parks came to us as a highly recognized navigator, and he flew all covert missions to Stockholm with us. It was his skill that got us through the thick clouds on our last combat flight. After the war he had a successful career at Westinghouse Electric. He is an outstanding citizen and a good family man, and I became fond of him during the time he served as navigator.

My second copilot was Lieutenant John Lancaster, who also joined us prior to our Stockholm flights. He and his wife Dot live in LaGrange, Georgia, where he retired after an outstanding career in forestry. Both his wife and mine grew up in Nashville and were classmates at Vanderbilt, and the four of us became close friends after the war was over.

Frank Stevenson flew the first twelve missions as tail gunner. None of our crew has heard from him after the war. George Weitzel, and Leonard Kanehl were original members of our crew. They were good men, but they were not needed on our Carpetbagger missions. The crew mourned the death of Kanehl several years ago.

My post war years began on the first Monday in September, 1945, when I reentered Vanderbilt. During my first two years there I had relied on odd jobs, my parents, and my brother Fleetwood for financial support. No longer. The GI bill paid my tuition, and the monthly check they sent me went a long way in paying other expenses. During my last two years I worked as a student instructor in surveying and mechanical drawing courses. This extra income helped me to thoroughly enjoy student life.

And it helped pay for dates.

Shortly after school began I fell deeply in love with a beautiful girl named Maureen Holt, who was also a student at Vanderbilt. It wasn't long before I knew that she was the only one for me. She accepted my proposal, and we were married on March 28, 1947, just a few days after my graduating Magna Cum Laude and becoming a charter member of Vanderbilt's Tau Beta Pi Honor Society.

I accepted employment with Humble Oil and Refining Company in Baytown, Texas. It was a great company to work for, and they paid their engineers well. Maureen and I had an exciting honeymoon for a week on our extended trip to Baytown. We stopped in Memphis, New Orleans, and Galveston.

The Baytown people were very friendly, I enjoyed my job, and Maureen had a good time teaching at Robert E. Lee High School. When we were free, we enjoyed driving down to the gulf with friends. I had seen a lot of oceans as a Carpetbagger pilot, but I had never gotten the opportunity to enjoy them. Our honeymoon seemed to last forever, and I thought I had found a place to settle down.

I had been with Humble for two years when one day I received a call to report to Dr. Franklin, the engineering supervisor. We had a friendly conversation, during which he praised my performance. Then he got to the point of the interview.

"I was wondering if you would be interested in a supervisory position," he began.

"Here?"

"No. It's with a subsidiary oil company in Caracas, Venezuela. As you know, the war caused a shortage of engineers, and they need an experienced engineer at the refinery."

I was reminded of the time Colonel St. Clair had asked me to volunteer to go to China. Like that decision, this one was easy.

"I appreciate the offer, Dr. Franklin, but I'm going to have to turn it down. I believe I've seen enough of the world already, and besides, I'm looking for a permanent home."

Dr. Franklin said he understood. He thanked me for my time, and I went back to my office. Then, two months later, I received an offer to move to Bayonne, New Jersey, where Standard Oil had its headquarters. Humble was like a minor league farm team to them, and Standard Oil preferred to bring in trained engineers. I considered it briefly, but knew that I had lived in the South too long to make such a transition. I finally decided to turn this offer down as well, knowing that doing so placed my career with Humble Oil in jeopardy.

I had received promotions and raises during my tenure at Humble. I loved my job, and I was fond of my fellow workers.

Moreover, I had invented important equipment for the company.[15] If I accepted the decisions of management, I was assured a bright future. But I was too much of a maverick to let someone else have that much control over my life.

I sat back and began to think about why I had become an engineer in the first place. My mother had encouraged me along that path, and I knew I had spent my college career fulfilling her wishes. But I remembered that during my high school years I had seriously thought of becoming a dentist. I thought about that some more, and found that my desire had not faded.

Over the next few days I considered the possibility of going back to school. I thought about what I would be giving up: a good job with a future, excellent pay, great working conditions, and friends. Besides, Maureen was happy.

But I also thought about how I would feel 25 years from now if I didn't try to do what I wanted to do. I would have lived out my mother's plans for me, not my own. And as a dentist I could be my own boss. . . .

A few days after I turned down the New Jersey transfer I walked through the front door of our apartment and found Maureen.

"Maureen, I've decided to go to dental school," I said. Her eyes widened. "Well, that's a surprise!"

"What do you think?"

"I think you ought to do whatever makes you happy," she replied. "Is it?"

"Yes."

We never regretted the decision.

Since my grades at Vanderbilt were high, I had no trouble gaining acceptance to the University of Tennessee School of

---

15 Humble allowed me and my immediate supervisor to share joint ownership of the patent. A year after I left the company, I released my share to my supervisor.

Dentistry, and I began my studies there in September, 1949—over 2 years since starting with Humble Oil. I went to school all year, and completed the 4 year program in three. Maureen taught school in Memphis, and I tutored high school and Memphis State students in math and science for extra money. I joined the Air Force Reserves, and was a weekend pilot of a C-46.[16] The GI bill paid my tuition again, gave me $125 a month since I was married, and helped me buy a home. I graduated in 1952 with top honors in my dental school class, and I had just turned twenty-nine when we moved to Nashville to begin my practice. It took three months for my office to be constructed, and during that time I kept busy as a substitute teacher in Nashville's public high schools. I enjoyed the students very much, and by the time my office was finished I was familiar with several people in the city.

I thoroughly enjoyed my 40 years as a dentist, but I must give credit where it's due. I will always love and appreciate my wonderful parents; without them I could have done none of what I've written about. Nor would my post war life have been meaningful without the love and support of my wife, Maureen. Both of us are proud of our daughter and son and their children.

This maverick was proud to be a Carpetbagger, and very proud to serve my country during World War II. I've had a variety of experiences over the course of my life, having done almost everything except author a book. Now that I've done that, what will I do next?

Count on it. I'll stay busy.

---

16 When I joined I was pleased to learn that Major White had made good on his promise of a promotion: I was a captain.